MINDFUL
ASTROLOGY

Inspiring | Educating | Creating | Entertaining

Brimming with creative inspiration, how-to
projects, and useful information to enrich your
everyday life, quarto.com is a favorite destination
for those pursuing their interests and passions.

First published in 2021 by Rock Point, an imprint of The Quarto Group
142 West 36th Street, 4th Floor, New York, NY 10018, USA
T (212) 779-4972 F (212) 779-6058 www.Quarto.com

Rock Point titles are also available at discount for retail, wholesale, promotional, and bulk purchase. For
details, contact the Special Sales Manager by email at specialsales@quarto.com or by mail at The Quarto
Group, Attn: Special Sales Manager, 100 Cummings Center Suite 265D, Beverly, MA 01915 USA.

10 9 8 7 6 5 4

ISBN: 978-1-63106-747-1

Library of Congress Control Number: 2020951546

Publisher: Rage Kindelsperger
Creative Director: Laura Drew
Managing Editor: Cara Donaldson
Senior Editors: John Foster and Katie Moore
Cover Design: Beth Middleworth
Interior Design: Laura Shaw Design

Printed in China

This book provides general information on various widely known and widely accepted practices that tend
to evoke feelings of strength and confidence. However, it should not be relied upon as recommending or
promoting any specific diagnosis or method of treatment for a particular condition, and it is not intended
as a substitute for medical advice or for direct diagnosis and treatment of a medical condition by a
qualified physician. Readers who have questions about a particular condition, possible treatments for that
condition, or possible reactions from the condition or its treatment should consult a physician or other
qualified health care professional.

MINDFUL
ASTROLOGY

Finding Peace of Mind According to
Your Sun, Moon, and Rising Sign

MONTE FARBER • AMY ZERNER

ROCK
POINT

Contents

INTRODUCTION

Mindful Astrology makes astrology simple to learn, fun to use, and . . . well, amazing! The word *astrology* is derived from *astro*, meaning "of the stars," and *logos*, meaning "the logical principle governing the cosmos," and for the past five thousand years, people have studied and passed down a major library's worth of writings about "star logic." With this book, we add our unique twenty-first-century take on astrology, providing all you need to know about your "sun sign" (what you tell people when they ask you, "What's your sign?"). This can help you in the following four important aspects of your life:

1. *love and relationships*

2. *work and career*

3. *wealth and success*

4. *wellness and mindfulness*

For each of the twelve signs of astrology's zodiac, we tell you about the life mission you have been given. How is this possible, you might ask? The answer is that astrology is a psychological language, a five-thousand-year-old personality-type system that proves what the Greek philosopher Heraclitus (*c.* 540–*c.* 480 BCE) said: "Character is destiny."

If you'd like to really fathom your friends and family, to be more aware and recognize what to expect of new people, and to see how cosmic influences work in human lives, then our *Mindful Astrology* is for you! By using the study of astrology as a mindful practice to recharge and align your mind, body, and spirit, you can become more fully yourself and live a richer life. Astrology reconnects us to our true take over inner powers and also helps us understand and empower others.

We have made this book to give you an effortlessly memorable and powerful new way of looking at yourself, those you care about, and the way you interact with your daily life. We have reimagined astrology as a psychological language, and in the following pages you will gain fascinating insights into not only yourself but also your partner, friends, and family.

Equipped with a free astrological birth chart (see page 20) and this book, you can become empowered and more aware of how you tick, your personal energy systems (we all have them!), the secrets to understanding individual character traits and the many challenges we all face in life. Most importantly, you will learn how to deal with these issues successfully.

Our system is designed to be a valuable resource for astrology beginners and professionals, too. We are the authors of other groundbreaking astrology books, some of which astrology enthusiasts may already have in their book collections. All of our books are valuable resources and are used by many astrology beginners, some of whom went on to become professional astrologers and who use our work to teach their classes.

· · SUN, MOON, AND RISING SIGNS · ·

Although *Mindful Astrology* is an easy-to-understand and in-depth look at each of the twelve zodiac signs, it is also much more than that. As important as your sun sign is, no astrologer can get a useful picture of who you are without knowing two crucial additional pieces of astrological information: your moon sign and your rising sign. This book empowers you to know yourself by giving you a three-dimensional picture of who you are from an astrological perspective, what we like to call your "celestial trilogy," by explaining your sun, moon, and rising signs. These are the three main cosmic energies that describe your personality. Once you know your sun, moon, and rising signs, you can explore how they work together to create *your* unique cosmic makeup. They are all equally important, and there is a constant flow and interaction between the three.

· · MINDFULNESS AND ASTROLOGY · ·

Now in the twenty-first century it is hard to retain anything in our brains for very long because new information, new inventions, new ways of doing things, and a "new normal" are thrust upon us each and every day. We have named our book *Mindful Astrology* because, unlike other astrology books, what you will learn in the following pages is designed to stay in your mind and add a new, powerful, and precise way to process information about yourself and others.

Mindfulness means being fully present in every moment—a noble goal, to be sure—and, to us, it also means filling our mind with information that actually helps us navigate daily life, not just transient chatter about things with little relevance to our lives or things that stir us up but which we can do little or nothing about. We each have only so many hours in the day, and so many days in our lives.

We can use mindfulness combined with astrology to "wake up" and connect with ourselves, improve our self-knowledge, and learn more about how we feel, think, and react. True mindfulness is characterized by self-acceptance and focusing on what is being experienced in the moment, not on the "what ifs," "should haves," "would haves," or "could haves" of our lives. The *ful* in the word *mindfulness* means being fully present. Mindfulness is also about knowing how to dig deep and find your inspiration, how to reflect on different perspectives, and how to make choice and change possible. We grow into better human beings by getting to know ourselves better and learning how to make better decisions.

To enhance this process, we have added tips to each of the twelve sun signs that are tailored to each sign's characteristics. They contain customized reminders and useful wellness tips based on your sun sign, which will help you restore and ground yourself to better deal with life's pressures and challenges. Finding peace of mind begins with self-reflection, to gain perspective on your goals, emotions, and reactions. By feeling your power to control yourself in the present moment, you can extend that power to affect all areas of your experience.

We have come to believe, without question, that the common denominator of all human-caused suffering is poor decision-making by those who choose to use their precious life to do ignorant, thoughtless, or hurtful things. These people ignore the danger signs and the rules of mindful, modern living and make choices that lead them to annoying, difficult, or potentially dangerous positions or situations where they cannot avoid damaged people and their damaging actions. With *Mindful Astrology* as your guide, you will not only better know yourself and those you care about, but you will have the tools you need to make better decisions and more mindfully navigate your daily life.

What Is Astrology and How Does It Work?

A STROLOGY, which has been around for thousands of years, is the study of how planetary positions relate to earthly events and people. Its long and rich history has resulted in a wealth of philosophical and psychological wisdom, the basic concepts of which we are going to share with you in the pages of this book. As we said in the introduction, the Greek philosopher Heraclitus said, "Character is destiny." Who you are—complete with all of your goals, tendencies, habits, virtues, and vices—will determine how you act and react, and thereby create your life's destiny. We think this saying is worth repeating to keep it at the front of your mind. Understanding astrology can help you better know yourself and those you care about. You will then be better able to use your free will to shape your life to your liking. Astrology is designed to help you become fully yourself. It can point out your strengths and weaknesses so that you can better accept yourself as you are and use your strengths to compensate for your weaknesses.

Virtually all Western music has been composed using variations of the same twelve notes. Similarly, the twelve sun signs of astrology are basic themes rich with meaning that each of us expresses differently to create and respond to the unique opportunities and challenges of our life. Real astrology teaches respect and tolerance because you see how alike we all are as much as how different we all are. Knowledge is power, and knowledge of astrology is empowering in the extreme!

The practice of astrology results from millennia of observation during which astrologers noticed, again and again, meaningful coincidences between the positions of the planets and events taking place on Earth. They were especially mindful of how these meaningful coincidences related to the horoscopes made for the rulers of the nations, because they felt that what happened to those rulers happened to their nations. When horoscopes started to be constructed for the rest of us, and not just the nobility, the seeds of democracy were first sown.

Astrology has evolved into a language-like system that lets us "read" the positions of the planets at the moment of our birth—the moment of our first breath, to be more precise. We visualize the taking of our first breath as if we are breathing in a sort of hologram of the matrix of energies caused by the interplay of the subtle gravitational and other energy waves emanating from the sun, moon, and the rest of the planets in our solar system. Whatever our manner of birth and first-drawn breath, we can interpret the map of this frozen moment in time and space to gain valuable insights into our individuality.

There are quite a few scientific theories that explain why astrology works. Our current favorite explanation for astrology's uncanny ability to give insight into a person's personality, and even its ability to forecast future events, is the chaos theory formulated by Benoit Mandelbrot (1924–2010). Mandelbrot coined the word *fractal* in 1975 for his newly formulated study of fractal geometry, which was expanded upon by Edward Norton Lorenz (1917–2008). Lorenz coined the term *deterministic chaos*; it is now known colloquially as "chaos theory," which concerns itself with non-linear systems—like the weather, brain function, and financial markets—and seeks to help understand how the effect of small changes or events can dramatically affect the results of seemingly unrelated events. The proven power of this "butterfly effect," the total interrelatedness of things, is a serious reminder to us all to be mindful of our thoughts and deeds, and that actions have consequences.

The theory of synchronicity, by pioneering Swiss psychologist Carl Jung, is a second explanation for how the energy patterns formed by planetary placements in space and symbolized in one's astrological birth chart (see page 20) can influence a person here on Earth. Jung's theory states that things occurring at the same moment form a relationship of significance, not actual causality. When you are born, you are a mirror of the energy patterns present at the time and place of your birth, including the energy patterns formed by the subtle gravitational waves given off by the sun, moon, and planets of our solar system. This pattern, symbolically represented by your astrology chart, can be read in a manner similar to the way a First Peoples shaman can look at the clouds in the sky or the movement of the leaves in the trees and read from these images signs of things to come and answers to questions.

A third explanation for how we can be influenced by the stars, whose chemicals we are all made from, is based on Albert Einstein's theory of relativity ($E = mc^2$), which at its heart proves that all matter is made of the same thing—that is, energy. If we, and everything else in the universe, are all made of the same energy, then at a most basic level we are all a part of one great whole. The ancient seers called the total sum of all the knowledge of the universe the Akashic Record, and today's seers, also known as quantum physicists, use the same concept and call it the Quantum Field. It is also possible that this Quantum Field of infinite knowledge can be accessed by a sincere seeker of knowledge, such as an astrologer reading a client's chart to help that client more successfully navigate the challenges of their life.

Perhaps this is the level that allows us to read not only an astrological birth chart, but also other people's minds, spiritual communications, psychic phenomena, and predictions of the future. Astrology can be used to predict one's future and more; however, to do so you need to thoroughly understand what is contained in the following pages, which will offer you a way of tapping into the magic that astrology has to offer and enchant you with the logic of the stars. To do this, we will use the rich symbolic language of the sun, moon, and rising signs of the zodiac to offer you guidance.

The word *zodiac* is taken from the Greek *zōidiakòs kýklos*, meaning "circle of animals," similar to a circus parade. The signs of the zodiac are derived from the star constellations that occupy the comparatively narrow band of outer space surrounding the Earth's equator. The planets move through the signs of the zodiac. When a planet is passing through a zodiac sign, that planet is said to be "in" the sign it is passing through. Each of the zodiac signs represents a different way of approaching the world. In astrology, the sign a planet is passing through modifies and blends its meaning with the energies signified by that planet.

WHAT ARE SUN SIGNS, MOON SIGNS, AND RISING SIGNS?

We all have had people ask us "What's your sign?" What they are *really* asking you for is what astrologers call your **sun sign**. It is called your sun sign because it is the sign of the zodiac the sun appeared to be in when you were born and took your first breath. An astrological birth chart (see page 20) is also known as a natal chart. It is also called your *horoscope*, from the Greek word *hora*, meaning "hour," and *scopus*, meaning "to look at," to give an overall meaning of "to look at the hour of your birth." In the psychological language of astrology, the sun represents our ego, our purpose, and the energy that animates us. Each of the twelve sun signs looks at the world from a very different perspective. Our sun sign, however, is just one piece of the puzzle of our personalities that can be "solved" by astrology's five-thousand-year-old accumulation of insights.

Only a fellow astrology buff or an astrologer will ever ask you what your **moon sign** is. This is the astrological sign where the moon was located at the moment of your birth, and it is equally important to astrologers because it represents your emotional intelligence—your ability to reflect upon life the way the moon reflects the light of the sun. And knowing which of the twelve signs the moon was in when you took your first breath can give astrologers like us (and soon, you) an insightful and nuanced picture of how you process emotions. But wait, there's more!

Your **rising sign**, also known as your **ascendant** (and abbreviated as **ASC** on a lot of computer-generated astrology reports), is simply the sign of the zodiac that was rising or ascending on the horizon at the moment of your birth. Knowing the sign that was rising on the horizon at the moment you took your first breath is the key to unlocking the mystery of how your spirit has chosen to project you into physical reality.

The traits of your rising sign are what others see when they look at you. This is why we are so excited to introduce you to yourself, to your rising sign, to the otherwise unknowable way that you appear to other people. For example, if you are born around sunrise, your rising sign will be the same sign of the zodiac you were born under and you will be a "double" Aries or Taurus—or whatever sign you are. When you are a double anything, what people see is pretty much what they get. Most people are not born at sunrise, however, so the way others perceive them is not an accurate portrait of who they are.

Not knowing your rising sign is like letting someone dress you while you keep your eyes closed. Only someone who knows you very well or loves you is going to understand who they are dressing and make sure that you are seen looking your best.

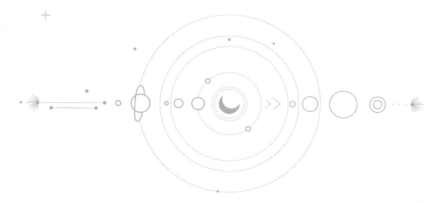

HOW TO CREATE AND READ
YOUR ASTROLOGICAL BIRTH CHART

Your astrological birth, or natal, chart helps clarify the particular issues you are dealing with, why you see things a certain way, and what you can do to improve your situation. Obtaining and reading your astrological birth chart is easy, and you can do it for free from many websites on the internet, such as Astrolabe (alabe.com) and Cafe Astrology (CafeAstrology.com). Our favorite website is Astrograph (astrograph.com/birth-chart.php).

The only information you will need to create a birth chart is your birthday and the time and place of your birth, which should all be recorded on your birth certificate. It is the law in most places that the time of birth be recorded and displayed on what is called the "vault copy" of your birth certificate (the birth certificate that is necessary to obtain a passport). A vault copy can usually be obtained by contacting the county clerk or other governmental agency tasked with recording births and deaths in the locality in which you were born.

Don't stress if you do not know your birth time, because the following chapters will still give you powerful guidance. If you do not know your birth time and have exhausted all efforts to obtain it (it's worth obtaining!), you can read about the twelve rising signs in the presence of someone you love and trust to be honest with you (remember, your rising sign is all about how others see you), and then narrow down potential rising signs to only a couple, no more. Then ask that trusted person to help you choose which rising sign best describes you.

Did you go to one of the websites and create your birth chart? If so, the astrological chart/natal chart/birth chart/horoscope that you should now have in hand looks like a pizza with twelve slices. We prefer the charts produced by websites that display this "pizza" as having equal slices. This pizza is arranged so that there is a horizontal line, sometimes marked "ASC," for "ascendant," and, in

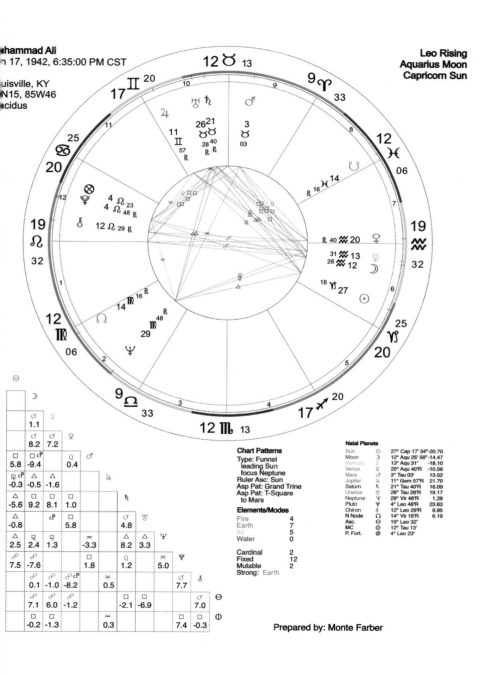

Muhammad Ali
n 17, 1942, 6:35:00 PM CST

uisville, KY
N15, 85W46
cidus

Leo Rising
Aquarius Moon
Capricorn Sun

Chart Patterns

Type: Funnel
leading Sun
focus Neptune
Ruler Asc: Sun
Asp Pat: Grand Trine
Asp Pat: T-Square
to Mars

Elements/Modes

Fire	4
Earth	7
Air	0
Water	5

Cardinal	2
Fixed	12
Mutable	2
Strong:	Earth

Natal Planets

Sun	☉	27° Cap 17' 34"	-20.70
Moon	☽	12° Aqu 25' 56"	-14.47
Mercury	☿	13° Aqu 31'	-18.10
Venus	♀	20° Aqu 40'R	-10.56
Mars	♂	3° Tau 03'	13.52
Jupiter	♃	11° Gem 57'R	21.70
Saturn	♄	21° Tau 40'R	16.09
Uranus	♅	26° Tau 28'R	19.17
Neptune	♆	29° Vir 48'R	1.28
Pluto	♇	4° Leo 48'R	23.63
Chiron	⚷	12° Leo 29'R	9.85
N Node	☊	14° Vir 16'R	6.19
Asc.	Θ	19° Leo 32'	
MC	Φ	12° Tau 13'	
P. Fort.	⊗	4° Leo 13'	

Prepared by: Monte Farber

an equal-slice-style chart, a vertical line, sometimes marked with an arrow and the initials "MC" for *Medium Coeli,* which is Latin for "middle of the heavens."

Each quarter of the pizza is further divided into three slices for a total of twelve. In astrology, each slice of the pizza represents a "slice of life," a piece of the hologram of energies that is each of us. Astrologers call these slices *houses* because, like a house, this is where the various "toppings" on your personal pizza, also known as the planets of your horoscope, call home.

The horizontal line represents the actual horizon, the surface of the Earth, at the moment you drew breath. All the symbolized planets below the horizon were behind the Earth at that moment and all the planets above the horizon were in the sky above you.

The planets, signs (think of them as twelve different kinds of cheese, one for each slice of the pizza), and the twelve houses of a person's birth horoscope are fixed and unalterable because your chart freezes in time the position of the twelve signs of the zodiac at the moment

you drew breath. The rising sign can be found on your horoscope wheel by looking at the symbol that is all the way over to the left on the horizontal horizon line.

Just as the sun rises in the east, so do the planets. The reason that east is on the left in a horoscope is because Western astrology started in the northern hemisphere and the horoscope pizza wheel is a symbolic representation of an ancient astrologer watching the planets, signs, and stars rise and set in the night sky, feet pointed south, so that east is on the left.

This incomparably wondrous and complex combination constantly moves due to the turning of the Earth. There are twelve signs revolving every twenty-four hours, so each sign is on the horizon for approximately two hours, depending on where in the world you were born. The constellations do not, however, vary in their order of succession. For example, the sign Aries is followed inevitably by Taurus, while the sign Libra is always the opposite or polarity of Aries and is placed directly across from Aries in the chart, whether Aries occupies the third, first, or any other house.

· · BIRTH CHART BASICS · ·

As you can see, birth charts contain a lot of information that can appear overwhelming. There are many glyphs, degrees, and other strange shapes that can be confusing. To cover each component of a birth chart would require a separate book; however, as we mentioned earlier, there are some things that you should be able to recognize in your birth chart printout to help you get the most out of this book.

We *highly recommend* holding yourself back from diving deep into it until you have read through all the chapters and become familiar with the important information we are sharing with you. This book is designed to give you a strong foundation that you can build upon if you want to learn more.

Most free charts will have your sun, moon, and rising signs printed somewhere on the chart (on the chart on page 21, it is in the upper right corner). Knowing your sun, moon, and rising sign is really all you need for the purposes of *Mindful Astrology*.

In addition, because astrology is a language written in symbols, many downloadable charts will give you a table of the glyphs, the symbols used to represent the planets and signs in your birth chart. For your reference, there is a chart opposite with the glyphs for the signs of the zodiac and the points and planets of any astrological chart. Each glyph in your birth chart represents a sign or planet or a point of reference.

Note: Chiron is a comet, not a planet, and neither is the North Node, South Node, nor anything else you see in a chart that is not the sun, moon, Mercury, Venus, Mars, Jupiter, Saturn, Uranus, Neptune, or Pluto. If you concern yourself only with your sun, moon, and rising signs as we explain them in this book, you will have a solid foundation upon which to build your astrological knowledge if and when you choose to learn about the rest of your chart.

· · YOUR CELESTIAL TRILOGY · ·

Understanding the combination of your sun, moon, and rising signs—what we call your Celestial Trilogy—helps you appreciate your character traits with curiosity, kindness, and graciousness, so that they will serve to strengthen your spiritual growth.

Unloved and neglected parts of ourselves act out until they get the healing and nurturing attention they require.

Developing an awareness of your Celestial Trilogy is a great place to start in being more mindful of your unique nature, feelings, and projections, as well as those of other important people in your life. Once you've discovered your sun sign, moon sign, and rising sign, continue with the next chapter!

PLANETS		ZODIAC SIGNS	
Sun	☉	Aries	♈
Moon	☽	Taurus	♉
Mercury	☿	Gemini	♊
Venus	♀	Cancer	♋
Mars	♂	Leo	♌
Jupiter	♃	Virgo	♍
Saturn	♄	Libra	♎
Chiron	⚷	Scorpio	♏
Uranus	♅	Sagittarius	♐
Neptune	♆	Capricorn	♑
Pluto	♇	Aquarius	♒
North Node	☊	Pisces	♓
South Node	☋		
Midheaven	M^C		
Ascendant	A^S		

Sun Signs

THE SUN in your astrological birth chart represents how you look out on the world. It is also closely tied to your ego and to how you are going to go about finding your purpose in life. The sun in a person's chart echoes the sun's function in our solar system: it is the central organizing principle of the various aspects of our personality, our sense of self and our ego.

The sign of the zodiac where the sun was on the day you were born gives you a strong inclination to uniquely express the basic themes associated with that zodiac sign. In this chapter and those about your moon (chapter 3) and rising signs (chapter 4), we have made it simple to understand the rich and intricate interplay of the various qualities associated with each of the twelve signs of the zodiac.

SIGN QUALITIES

Cardinal ➔ | *Fixed* ◊ | *Mutable* ≈

Ancient astrologers further enhanced the precise meaning of each of the signs by assigning to each a **quality** classification of either **cardinal**, **fixed**, or **mutable** and associated four zodiac signs with each quality.

CARDINAL SIGNS ➔

The four cardinal signs are the signs whose first day corresponds with the first day of each season, **Aries** (spring), **Cancer** (summer), **Libra** (fall), and **Capricorn** (winter). These four cardinal signs are said to have the quality of being goal-oriented. People born with the cardinal signs prominent in their charts are more likely to want to "climb the mountain" they have decided to climb.

FIXED SIGNS ◊

The four fixed signs follow the cardinal, goal-oriented signs, and are inclined to "fix," or keep in place, the actions initiated by the cardinal signs. The fixed signs are **Taurus**, **Leo**, **Scorpio**, and **Aquarius**. In astrology, the fixed signs are known as the stubborn signs. Getting them to deviate from a course of action requires a lot of effort, except when circumstances force them to admit they have made a mistake.

MUTABLE SIGNS ≈

The four mutable signs follow the fixed, stubborn signs and precede the cardinal, goal-oriented sign that begins the next season. The mutable signs must therefore be flexible and able to bridge one season to the next. The mutable signs are **Gemini**, **Virgo**, **Sagittarius**, and **Pisces**. The mutable signs also have goals, but they accomplish them by being flexible and adjusting their course when they find information that appeals to them at the moment.

In addition to cardinal, fixed, and mutable qualities, the signs of the zodiac are also assigned to four **elements**: Earth, fire, water, and air. We will look more closely at these four elements and how they add yet another layer of nuance to each sign later in chapter 3 (see page 142). For now, let's look at the major themes in the approach to living of each of the twelve sun signs.

We have included in-depth information and guidance for each sign about love and relationships, work and career, and wealth and success, describing for you the tendencies of the past, and predicting present and future inclinations.

See if you can avoid letting your mind play its usual game, which is to be vigilant for any information that causes you fear. If you really want to learn more about your true self, you must remember the first lesson of learning anything: read and absorb the information in a state of relaxed, mindful attention.

Note: The start and end dates for the twelve signs given in this or any other astrology book are approximations. Depending on the year, the sun can enter or leave a sign before or after the dates our book gives you. Therefore, check your chart to be sure of your sun sign if you were born a day or two before or after a change of zodiac sign.

SUN IN ARIES

(MARCH 21–APRIL 19)

QUALITY *Cardinal* → | **ELEMENT** *Fire* 🔥

Although Aries was also known as Mars, the god of war, for both the Romans and the Greeks, not every Aries likes to fight. Some Aries emulate the feisty, aggressive ram, the symbol of the sign, and some are more like the sheep, even though simply going along to get along is not healthy for those born during this time—Aries are known to channel their aggression inward, which can cause depression.

The fight-flight-freeze human instinct is a basic characteristic of Aries. If you feel even slightly afraid, the emotion makes you lash out, run away, or become paralyzed with panic. You must stay spontaneous and not let natural fears cause self-doubt or self-defeating behavior or freeze you into inaction, thereby causing even more self-doubt.

Aries have great instinctive faculties and are capable of amazing progress when they can be a pioneer in some area of expertise. You are usually not afraid to venture from the beaten track, and seek new ideas that are inspired by many sources.

Aries rarely read for relaxation, but they do enjoy reading useful information when they are researching their latest project. You prefer short, to the point, and even newsworthy material rather than long, involved tomes. You like to keep abreast of the times rather than reminisce about the past or speculate about the future. You are quite definite in your opinions; you never straddle any issue. You know what you like (and can be a bit bossy). Others may wheedle you into trying something new, but you will never repeat it if you do not enjoy it.

Enthusiasm is a prominent and attractive feature of your personality. In general, you are good-natured, warmhearted, and upbeat. You seldom indulge in pessimistic moods because you detest doom and gloom. When others appear depressed, you start telling funny stories that can make them laugh.

Rather than hesitate when things have to be done, you perform necessary tasks quickly. Even if the results are not satisfactory, you seldom have regrets. You prefer to forget about your mistakes.

Because you know what you want, the best course of action is to pursue your goals as if you have already succeeded. You can rarely be accused of indecision. You usually get things on the first go, and it is not a good idea for you to second-guess yourself. Also, you won't follow advice if it goes against your preconceived ideas.

You like to relax between bursts of activity. Often you find that being physical is the best means of obtaining mental rest. You enjoy the scenic beauty of nature and outdoor activities. When you are feeling social, you like parties where you can lead a group in a game. You are generous, and you prefer to gift your favors to those who you know personally.

In giving advice to others, you can be quite assertive. You can be diplomatic when necessary, but when you need facts, you prefer to ask direct questions. You can get from place to place and thought to thought quickly, and appear to others to be always on the go and constantly busy.

You often get pleasure out of teasing those whom you like a lot. Occasionally, someone who has not taken the time to get to know you can get the impression that you are rude. It is obvious when someone interests you: your eyes seem to light up, as though an electric switch has been snapped on inside you.

You are strong and passionate in love and capable of deep devotion. You are considerate of family members, although at times you appear self-absorbed when you are actually thinking about how to help them. You are attached to your home but also need regular outside stimulation. Your interest in new projects makes you impetuous, often starting more projects than you can finish, which is why you cannot bear to be tied down to routine domestic obligations.

· · LOVE AND RELATIONSHIPS · ·

You bring the theme of "pioneering" to your relationships. You usually are the first to make your move and are not afraid to jump in. If you are in a committed relationship, you often need to break new ground and take it to the next level. You will not be content if things are not moving forward.

If you are looking for a relationship, it usually will not come to you because you enjoy everything involved with going looking for it, especially in places where you have never been before, through travel, or by pushing beyond your usual comfort zone. You like it when you can test and prove yourself and your relationships in new ways.

If you do not have a relationship, it may be because you fear that having one means giving up your individuality and personal freedom, or you may like your life the way it is. You may also feel, rightly or wrongly, that you have a lot of work to do on yourself, or your career, before you can get involved with someone else's life.

You may have to overcome some very conflicted feelings about whether or not you have the right to look out for your own interests in a relationship. You do have this right. The best relationship for you is one where you can be yourself without restrictions. You must be able to speak your mind forcefully, even if your partner does not want to hear it. This is why Aries need to have partners who are strong enough to be themselves while you are being yourself—no overly sensitive people need apply.

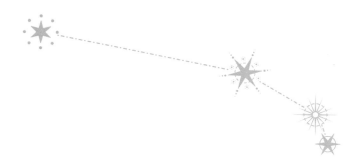

Don't let your fears protect you to the point that you live your life alone, unless that is really what you want. All your fears, and those of your partners, must be faced, understood, and dealt with, or they will undermine your relationships.

Difficulties in relationships may be a result of issues surrounding honesty. Either you or your partners may have been too honest or not honest enough, or the relationships of those you grew up with or care about could have been hurt or destroyed by dishonesty.

Associate with those who support you and your dreams of the future. Allow all those you encounter to respond to the real you. To be surrounded by interesting, self-assured, and admiring friends you must first become secure enough to know what you like and dislike.

Remember, having good self-esteem does not mean thinking and acting like you have no faults. It is possible and very beneficial for you to be aware of your faults. We all have faults; being aware of them is the first step to learning how to cope with them.

To have the healthiest relationships, be mindful to give voice to all your original ideas and feelings. Even if you end up butting heads a bit, it is a good idea to get everything out in the open. Anything other than honesty and directness is just not going to work for you.

· · WORK AND CAREER · ·

For an Aries, issues of honesty can make or break a work situation. Always try to be as honest as you can without exposing yourself to unnecessary trouble. Being too honest or headstrong can sometimes be as problematic as being dishonest, so strive for balance.

The challenge may sometimes be that other people are dishonest, or too honest, and you might be drawn into the mess they are making. If so, make sure that any dishonesty is dealt with appropriately. Thinking that you alone need to defend another person can backfire, because you may do it more forcefully than the situation warrants.

WELLNESS AND MINDFULNESS FOR ARIES

Aries rules the head and the face. Aries people should be mindful of what is going on in their head—especially feelings of stress caused by fear, missed deadlines, and lost opportunities. Stress strongly influences what is going on in the body and makes Aries prone to headaches.

Little "time-outs" are good for an Aries: hot baths, five minutes in a hammock—these will work wonders to heal and rejuvenate. Self-massage with a focus on the forehead and the temple area would be especially calming and helpful.

Be careful to extricate yourself from sticky situations as quickly, but as carefully, as you can.

Your actions need to show all of those concerned in a work project that you are honest and your own person, not part of any clique. Act like the pioneer you are and go off on your own and work by, or for, yourself if necessary. Do your job as if you owned your company. It is important that you be able to work without too much interference.

In the recent or distant past, you may have demonstrated to yourself that you have the ability to work well with others, helping them to shine, and were content to share the glory with the group; however, it is good for you to lead. You have something unique to contribute to any team, and if they do not let you do so, you must take your contribution elsewhere. Your innovative ideas are a rare commodity that must be valued and acted on.

If you cannot get over feeling impatient with the pace of others or with the speed of your career's advancement, then why try to deny it?

Remember, Aries = honesty. However, avoid being too honest about this. It is good to test the accuracy of your beliefs by stating them forcefully and seeing whether others can challenge them. Just keep in mind that not everyone has the time or the strength to play this game with you too often.

It does get a bit lonely when you are committed to doing things in your own unique way. Those who are insecure about their own abilities may see your display of willpower as a threat. However, when others see that you know what you are doing, they will understand your actions for what they are—the actions of an uncompromising individualist who follows their instincts.

You may find it necessary to stick up for your own interests and put yourself first. Any arguments you find yourself in again and again, either with the same person or with different people, are a sign that you may be wasting your time and energy explaining yourself when you could be blazing new and exciting career trails.

· · WEALTH AND SUCCESS · ·

To be more successful, imagine you are a pioneer starting out on an adventure to seek your fortune. You may not know the details, but you know you are on your way. Take action to investigate businesses you can start yourself, without necessarily giving up the support of the job you have until the new source of income can sustain you.

Don't always reveal to everybody what you are trying to achieve; often they will not understand your goals and motives. They will view challenges as obstacles and not as the stepping-stones to success that all lessons are. This will get in your way and slow you down. Share your ideas only with those who have proven they are as honest as you and worthy of your trust.

As mentioned earlier, Aries like to be the first at something, so inventions and new ways of doing things come naturally to you. Wealth and success can come to you from ideas that are related to you

personally and events in your daily life. You may get an idea because of an experience or a need that you have and translate it creatively into something that can benefit you and others.

Wealth and success can also come to you as a result of your own efforts. They are probably not going to be given to you. You might have to do everything yourself, but that is a good thing. Focus on your desires. Start from where you are and use all the resources you have available to you.

You will succeed in proportion to the amount of time and energy you have been putting out to *do* your best and not to *be* the best. Doing your best energizes you and everyone you meet. Trying to be the best puts too much emphasis on forces that are beyond your Aries control.

If there are young people in your life, accept them as the unique individuals they are. In return, they will make you feel better about how well you have done for yourself and for them. Be a shining example to them of what it means to be your own person.

Although it may feel odd at first, make a regular time each day to love yourself more and appreciate your good traits and accomplishments. Most of us are too hard on ourselves because of the misguided notion that this will spur us on to be better and work harder. Loving yourself is essential to having the wealth and success you desire.

Aries are competitive, and as a result of competing, they are favored to receive awards and win contests where individual skills are involved, rather than matters of chance. You work hard to be recognized for your accomplishments as an individual and really want your abilities to shine and pay off handsomely.

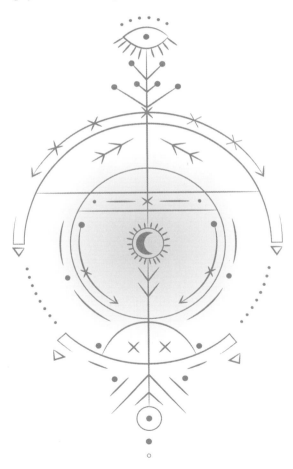

SUN IN TAURUS

(APRIL 20–MAY 20)

QUALITY *Fixed* ◊ | **ELEMENT** *Earth* ⊕

Taureans value an established, stable, middle-of-the-road approach
to life. Not likely to get caught up in the latest trend, they believe
in being themselves. Taureans need to understand that being true
to their values does not mean they should be afraid to change their
situation, ideas, or habits once in a while.

Your calm disposition keeps you from appearing annoyed when
others become excited. However, at times your patience gives out. Only
under extreme provocation do you lose your temper. You do your best
to hold back your wrath with iron willpower because you know how
devastating your anger can be.

You make every effort to remain serene because you do not like to be
in an atmosphere of discord. Occasionally, you go to extremes of personal
strength and endurance to achieve this. One of your favorite methods is
to agree with others when you notice a situation becoming tense.

You have a carefully developed sense of allegiance. Your love is most
often based on reality, rather than idealistic. You do not believe in
sacrificing for an abstract goal, but you do not hesitate to risk all for
the one you love. You probably enjoy the companionship of your mate
far more than spending time with relatives and friends. Usually you
are on the best terms with everyone, but your free time belongs to
experiencing the pleasures of life.

When well directed, your determination can be invaluable. But
when misdirected, your stubbornness and resistance to making big
changes can become a stumbling block and cause you to put up with
things that you would be better off letting go of.

You listen carefully to what others have to say, and you remember what you hear. You are deliberate and methodical in your thoughts and deeds. This gives you an exceptional sense of authority in affirming or contradicting others.

For rest, relaxation, and recreation, you prefer your home or a beautiful, familiar place. When possible, however, you like to travel, provided you can be assured of little luxuries. On any journey, you like to be accompanied by someone who provides assistance and enjoyable companionship and shares your taste for comforts.

You are fond of beauty in all forms, especially beautiful flowers, lavish decorations, and probably a pet or two. You love good food and any opportunity to show off your talent in selecting interesting cuisine. The desire for delicious meals can sometimes result in unnecessary food waste and also prove expensive.

Because the sign Taurus rules material wealth, you are likely to depend on the good things in life to maintain your peace of mind and contentment. Usually your attitude is calm, your viewpoint inflexible, and your disposition placid. As a result, you are often challenged to deal with changeable or impulsive people.

In a career, you can do well when you work with an associate, or with a single client at a time. This characteristic is at its best in connection with occupations such as private teaching, design, or investments. Financial security means a lot to you, so you are especially desirous of a guaranteed income from investments, royalties, or an estate.

Being able to acquire money easily, you spend it just as readily. Nevertheless, your understanding of practical matters and human nature affords you your own brand of financial wizardry that enables you to be an excellent financier or investor.

Many Taurus natives have musical abilities. It should be easy for you to develop as a vocalist or an instrumentalist, because you enjoy melodies and rhythms for their own sake. Music will be more important to you than to most people and you will benefit from listening to music you like, actually drawing strength from it.

When it comes to fashion, you look for value in materials, authenticity, and exclusive design. You are able to attract affluence through your own efforts, through gifts, or in bequests from people and entities that want to reward your dependability.

· · LOVE AND RELATIONSHIPS · ·

It is very important that anyone you partner with shares your tastes and desires in life. If you like deluxe comfort and your partner likes to camp out, there may eventually be a parting of the ways.

If you stay true to what you believe, you will be fulfilled, whether you have a relationship or not. Conversely, if you are going against what you know to be right, things are not going to go well with or without a partner.

If you do not have a relationship but want one, the delay may be caused by the fact that you are too stubborn or are so afraid of stubborn people that you avoid anyone who appears stubborn to you.

Another reason for the delay may be your present attitude and past experiences regarding money, possessions, and the resources available to you to live the way you want to live.

Partnered or not, be mindful of the way you, your partner, or a love interest have dealt with money and possessions in the past and how that past situation could now be affecting your love life. If you have commingled your resources with those of a partner and things are not going smoothly, you may have to separate out what is yours to put things back on an even footing.

Seek a relationship where you value each other because of who you are, not just because of what you have. Many wonderful relationships that could have been never come to pass because some people look at potential love interests as if they were potential financial backers.

A relationship lasts when it is a union of two independent people who are secure in as many ways as possible. Being with people only because of what they can offer you and not for who they are will not lead to lasting happiness, and Taurus likes things that last. We have seen that those who are cheap with their money and possessions are cheap with their ability to love and show love.

You have to be patient with your partners, at least those who deserve your patience, and they have to be patient with you. Be practical. Make a plan. With issues of love, patience is truly a virtue. Take things slowly. When stressful times come—and they always do—and you both are trying your best to deal with it, then you should allow for a bit of thoughtless behavior on each other's part. No one is perfect.

You most likely will not break up easily because Taurus copes well with difficult situations. However, if you keep a relationship going longer than you should and then you decide to end it, the emotional toll on you both will be far greater than if you broke up earlier. Leaving or making big changes will be even more difficult for Taurus sun people who also have the moon and/or their rising sign in Taurus.

Taurus loves material comforts, so if you are well-off, you are not likely to split from your partner if it involves splitting your resources and

WELLNESS AND MINDFULNESS FOR TAURUS

TAURUS knows how to sustain effort in matters that concern talent, security, values, and finances. They do not like to quit, even when they should. Therefore, learning how to let go is one of the most important mindfulness lessons for Taurus.

Bulls should sing or chant to nourish their neck and throat, larynx, vocal cords, tonsils, thyroid, chin, lower jaw, ears, and tongue—all parts of the body ruled by Taurus. They can benefit from writing a letter to themselves advising themselves to let go of situations that have gone on too long.

diminishing your lifestyle significantly. If you lack money, it will also be difficult to leave your present situation. If you think you need to do so, start saving up for the fateful day when you will make your big move.

·· WORK AND CAREER ··

For Taurus, forces causing movement in your career may not immediately be apparent. See the developments in your career as being like the first flowers of spring—though things sometimes appear gray and cold, there is movement beneath the frozen surface. You may not realize how beautiful life is going to be until things start popping up like those first flowers.

Great rewards are possible for you, in the form of you being valued for your abilities, steady hand, and consistent contributions. It is good to be mindful of preparations for promotions and bonuses to come, rather than of the promotions and bonuses themselves. Do not stray from the course you know to be the right one for you.

It will be difficult for you to do your job properly if you are not being paid what you believe you are worth. If that is the case, then you must either try to get a raise or investigate other more lucrative options. Once again, it is not easy for Taurus natives to make big changes: remember that you can use your legendary Taurus bull-like strength to leave rather than simply to endure your current situation. The easier it is for a Taurus to make big changes, the more they have progressed on a spiritual level.

If you have troubles at work, reflect on whether you or someone else is being greedy or whether too much importance is being put on a situation that does not merit it. It would be equally valuable for you

to discover whether a potentially profitable or otherwise valuable situation is being wasted for lack of proper attention. Leave new business to others until you are sure that existing situations have been dealt with properly.

A career where experiencing the finer things in life would be part of your compensation would be a dream come true. If you are younger, it could benefit you to take an entry-level position in a career connected with providing luxuries or services for the well-to-do. If you are older, consulting work would be a good choice.

Work in the financial realm of the business world could benefit Taurus. Research how financial resources can be properly allocated, used, and developed. Conserve and be conservative. Make a note of all obstacles you believe are standing in your way. March steadily on and gather strength from your accomplishments. Later on, you will be glad that you took this time to assess your situation and consolidate the benefits of past efforts. Doing so will expose you to opportunities that you would otherwise have never imagined were so close to home.

Your gift is helping to strengthen and consolidate things at work, rather than doing things differently. Slow and steady is the way to proceed for Taurus. It is the best way to increase your power and prestige. Stick to a well-described routine or the plan of a superior.

Occupations where you could excel include transportation, construction, conservation, landscaping, farming, engineering, design, tech, and the fine arts—especially sculpture, design, fashion, and music.

· · WEALTH AND SUCCESS · ·

Before they take the time and expend the resources to attain a goal, Taurus natives generally have to work on a plan involving hard work and patience, or else they will not value their achievement highly.

Be pragmatic and take what you can get. Usually, if you have not deviated from the plan you made, you can expect to succeed.

It is always best for you to conserve your resources. Put money regularly in safe and secure investments and you will do better than you would by taking chances. Risk-taking and gambling are not for the sign of Taurus.

You may, however, be seen by others as attracting luck. You may gain by inheritance, win a contest where the prize is awarded for perseverance or beauty, or succeed in a situation where you have to keep renewing your entry again and again. You could also be recognized for sticking with something others had given up on. Also favored are matters involving art, beauty, long-term investments, farming, gardening, and all other pursuits where your ability to make things look good is crucial.

Like the slow, steady turning of the Earth, your persistent efforts to attain wealth and success will pay off. You can be rewarded in proportion to how true to your value system you have been. Expect some luck as the result of good planning and endurance on your part. You have the ability to think of many ways to create money. Your patience is one of your most valuable assets.

Be practical and conserve what you have so that you will have enough when you need it. What resources you have saved for the future will stand you in good stead. This does not always have to be money or wealth in the material sense. What you consider necessary for your own success is what is important. The strength of your self-confidence and faith is as important as any material resource.

Appreciate the resources you have as the blessings and rewards they are. Feel that you are on the fast track to wealth and success.

Making a time each day to give thanks for what you have can make you even more successful. Do not concentrate on what you lack or what you desire, as that depletes your Taurus strength. Try, instead, to want what you have, for then you immediately have what you want. This is not silly wordplay; it is powerful thought programming, also known as an affirmation. Saying this sets up a calm strength that resonates with your future experience of getting what you want.

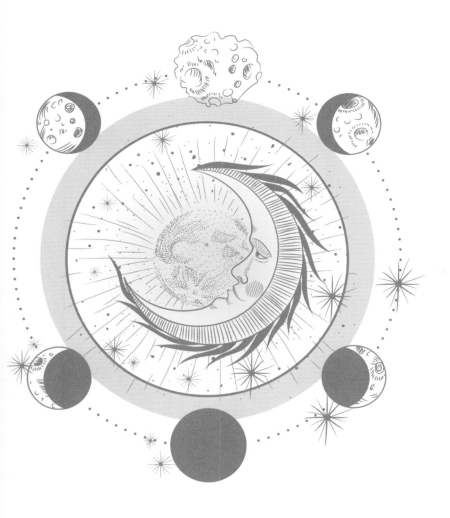

SUN IN GEMINI

(MAY 21–JUNE 20)

QUALITY *Mutable* ≈ | **ELEMENT** *Air* ≋

Geminis hunger for information from all sources: the internet, books, television, social media, newspapers, magazines, and especially word of mouth, the reason this sign is associated with gossip. They will do practically anything to avoid being bored—which, to a Gemini, is a fate almost worse than death.

Because your mind works quickly, you can understand any subject. This instinct enables you to keep ahead of others and also manifests as your seeming to act like two (or more) different people as you explore the various aspects of just about anything. Only those who take the time to get to know you will understand that you are not contradicting yourself: you are articulating your new understanding of whatever you are applying your lightning-fast mind to.

You enjoy being among articulate, well-informed people. You have the ability to absorb and assimilate what you hear and see, and it is easy for you to adjust yourself to new trends and social mores.

Rarely do you allow yourself to feel bored. You change your routine when things are dull, and you usually find enough interests to keep you occupied every day. A home filled with communication gadgets, books, mementos, collections, and hobbies is one of your primary requirements.

You are capable of appreciating abstract theories with your curious mind, and you like to keep up with timely topics and current events. You don't need to spend many hours in concentrated study. Knowledge comes to you without effort, because you have a knack for gaining information through casual conversation, browsing the web, reading, watching a screen or two, listening to the radio, and scanning the print media, usually all at the same time. No one is a better multitasker than a Gemini.

You derive exhilaration and stimulation from matching wits with others. That is why you are seldom at a loss for an appropriate answer to almost any question. Your repartee amuses relatives, friends, acquaintances, and even your neighbors. You are quite free in the expression of your ideas and open to the ideas of others, even if you don't follow their advice.

You like short visits. After a brief call, you take your leave with a smile and a few amusing remarks. Matters that pertain to relatives, friends, and neighbors are of interest to you. You like to help celebrate their birthdays. You commemorate anniversaries in an original way. When you send a gift, it is usually accompanied by a short, meaningful message that you composed yourself. Frequently your present is created by hand with a manual skill, such as calligraphy, computer graphics, woodworking, designing, or one of the decorative crafts.

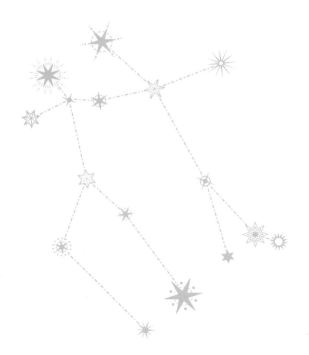

Your mind is constantly at work. You would do well as a teacher, sales expert, promoter, or marketing/advertising specialist. The ability to put thoughts into words is a strong factor in your success.

A set routine does not appeal to you. You are happiest when you have to handle several tasks simultaneously, because you can change your ideas and actions rapidly. This flexibility is an admirable trait, as it usually helps you arrive at perceptive and savvy evaluations of people and events. However, you sometimes lose sight of essentials, or you can be so mercurial that it borders on instability. That is why you need an occupation that can serve as mental ballast.

Though you are self-reliant, you do not mind winning favors or honors without working for them. Your social sense allows you to enjoy the company of others anywhere that friends and neighbors congregate. Wherever you go, you are welcome for your friendly disposition.

Because your nature is adaptable, you can associate with almost any type of person. You are tolerant and usually considerate, though you can sometimes ignore the fact that there is a real live human being in front of you with needs that must be addressed. These attributes appeal to

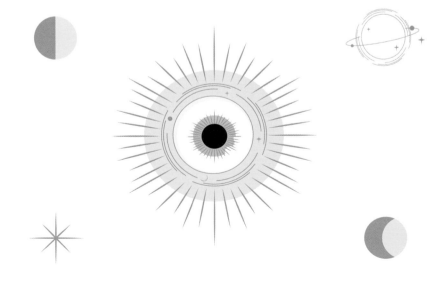

those who need an optimistic and capable associate. In a marriage you have the same gifts because you believe in freedom and flexibility for your mate as well as for yourself.

You are usually a remarkably considerate neighbor. To show your sympathy in times of trouble you call personally, write friendly notes, supply special treats, send a soothing email, or drop off a collection of books and magazines that are interesting and inspiring.

Your attitude is to enjoy the good things in life now and from day to day. You need to space your activities so that you have ample time for rest and leisure instead of being overworked and suffering from the insomnia that comes with knowing you have more work to do than time to do it in.

Your keen Gemini sense of humor enables you to perceive the ludicrous. Often you amuse your acquaintances and relatives by imitating their laughable habits, or you tease them by playing practical jokes.

·· LOVE AND RELATIONSHIPS ··

You may find that you are sometimes interested in more than one person at the same time, even if you or they are in a committed relationship, or more than one person is interested in you. There may be quite a difference in your age, station in life, or educational background and that of your new partner(s).

If you do not have a love relationship, it is important that, even when you are flirting, you present yourself to others in a consistent manner. Avoid appearing two-faced or superficial, or seeming impatient or desperate. Talking about marriage on the first date is a no-no.

If you are not in a relationship and want one (or two), you might find one through your siblings or other relatives. You would be likely to meet someone interesting while taking classes or on-the-job training. A relationship might come to you in a place you ordinarily take for granted, such as where you work, go to school, or go shopping, or even on your way to or from such a place. Online dating would work for you because someone's ability to communicate is very important to you.

If you are in a relationship, problems may result from difficulties relating to your partner, or vice versa. There may be too much of a difference between you; upbringing, schooling, religion, type of work, friends, work ethic, basic philosophy, and a host of other differences may have driven a wedge between you. One or both of you may be feeling completely misunderstood. If you want to keep the relationship going, you must communicate that clearly. Nonverbal clues and playing games will not help you.

For things to work out, you must make an effort to relate to each other and understand your differences. When a person is with a Gemini, they have to understand that there are actually two (or more) people inside you. Your ability to understand other points of view so well can backfire and make you seem like you want to have things both ways. In arguments your partner may point this out or use other harsh language to catch you up on your seeming contradictions.

You may be so busy that a romantic relationship can suffer from separation anxiety and therefore manifest too much "brother and sister" energy and not enough romance and intimacy. If that is so, communicate your affection, show your desire, and make time for romantic interludes, no matter what.

Geminis have the gift of the gab, but avoid gossip if you do not want to spend your time dealing with hurt feelings. Choose your words carefully and make sure you are saying what you mean. Two people can hear the same words but interpret them in radically different ways. Geminis in particular have to be careful what they write in emails.

It is important that you keep a private journal. Seeing your thoughts on paper will help you clarify many areas of your life, not just love and relationships. The written word has power, especially for a Gemini.

Your Gemini personality is used to relating to many people at the same time, either in person or via telephone, text, email, social

networking, or otherwise. Jealousy may arise because you are flirting, not home, or not paying a lot of attention to others around you.

Problems may also arise because you, your partner, or both of you might be acting like two different people. This makes trust difficult and gives rise to fear and suspicion. It is important that you both know and trust each other.

If you both trust and respect each other and there are still difficulties, the problem may be that you are not communicating well. Both of you must listen as if the other might be saying something important. Avoid the tendency to think about what you are going to say next when your partner is talking. Keep talking to each other even if you get into an argument.

Reading, writing, learning, and growing as a person in maturity, knowledge, and understanding must be an important part of any relationship you are involved in. Taking courses or developing your skills together can improve your bond.

· · WORK AND CAREER · ·

If your work or career is boring or not challenging enough, the best way to deal with it is to stay at your job while planning to change jobs or careers. The time you could spend daydreaming about your new line of work may actually help you find ways to improve your present job, and you might even find changing jobs unnecessary.

For this to happen, you have to be able to use everything you know in a display of your versatility. Use your existing connections to advance yourself. Any discomfort you feel with this reveals the amount of work you will have to do before you are able to advance yourself.

Even if your work is satisfying to you, there will be times when you may want to branch out or do a second job. For a Gemini, sometimes doing two jobs is easier and more beneficial than doing only one. You enjoy taking courses, going to school, or having a job where you are constantly learning.

Be mindful about your punctuality: it is important that you are on time to all appointments or you might miss an opportunity. Gemini versatility can lead you to be scattered in your attention, and finding keys and papers could delay you.

Check all of your travel plans thoroughly and allow yourself plenty of time to meet those with whom you have appointments. Let them be the ones who are late, not you. Even traveling to and from those appointments might be beneficial in some way.

It is unreasonable to expect people to help your career until they know you and your abilities. Get to know them and they will help you. Your rising sign (see chapter 4) will give you insight into how you appear to be two different people. When you understand that, a self-presentation problem can become a valuable asset.

Some people won't understand that every Gemini can appear to be two people, or won't understand your motives regarding your network of contacts. You can educate these people or avoid them altogether. Making the right connections will teach you many things about people

WELLNESS AND MINDFULNESS FOR GEMINI

GEMINI knows how to adjust and improvise their style of communication to deal with fluctuations, and they can adapt themselves to their environment. Therefore, learning how to craft a unique set of core beliefs is one of the most important mindfulness lessons for Gemini.

Geminis tend to have a sensitive nervous system; therefore, they need to make sure to get enough sleep and can facilitate drowsiness by doing relaxation meditations before bedtime. Also, they should be frequently rotating their wrists and relaxing their hands during work.

you may have thought you did not like. In this way, you will get close to the universal ideal of loving all.

Occupations that you would do well in are communications, publicity, journalism, accounting, computers, and anything requiring you to use your highly active mind as you meet a lot of new people on a regular basis.

No matter what you do, it is always a good idea to streamline your work and make sure that the path to your career goals is clear. Study as much as you can about your job and where you want to be in three years. Become part of information exchanges so that you can stay abreast of the latest information and advances in your industry.

Be mindful of any prejudices and preconceived notions and do your best to rid yourself of them. Everyone has them, but a Gemini is so all over the map with their concentration and self-image that core beliefs can often get lost in the shuffle. It is important to look beneath the surface of people and their actions to understand why they are acting the way they are. You will usually find that it is nothing personal; they are only trying to better their own situation.

·· WEALTH AND SUCCESS ··

It is possible for a Gemini to be wealthy and not feel wealthy. In many ways, you very well could be better off than you were in the past, yet arriving at this point has taken its toll and opened your eyes to new aspects of life. Your sharp mind makes you as aware of what you lack as of what you have. It is important to concentrate on what you have, however.

If you do not learn to control your overactive mind, you may feel anxious about attaining more wealth and success. This can make you feel moody, dejected, and depressed from time to time. This issue is usually the product of an undisciplined mind.

Learn all you can about accumulating and managing money. Reading books and taking courses would be very beneficial. You might also ask a successful sister, brother, or relative to give you advice. Whatever you learn, putting money into an account where it can work for you should become a part of your everyday routine.

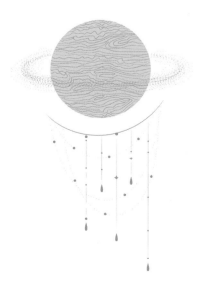

Investments related to communications, publishing, transportation, schools, and education can benefit you. Whatever you invest in, you should get out and see for yourself what they do. You may be told that investing is about passion, but that is not necessarily true in the case of Gemini investors.

It is especially crucial that you know the basic important information about any investment advisors. You would be amazed at how many people skip this step and are surprised when the advisor turns out to be less skilled and sometimes less honest than you expected.

There is potential for your receiving recognition, gifts, prizes, and awards from activities involving relatives, neighbors, schools, and communities. Quizzes, puzzles, riddles, or contests related to famous quotes or everday products and services will be most likely to bring you rewards. Appreciate the wealth of your eyesight, manual dexterity, and ability to communicate, if you are fortunate enough to have these gifts.

Envy is a waste of time, and this is especially true for Geminis. We all have our challenges. Yours is to accept how much better off you are than many other people and to improve without belittling yourself for the things you have not yet accomplished.

To be more successful, it is important that you get enough information to emulate and even speak like someone who is successful. Acting "as if" will prepare you for the future. Too many people think that wealth and success will solve all their problems and refuse to realize that they bring in a whole host of problems most people cannot conceive of. This is why most people do not attain them.

Increased wealth and success for you, a Gemini, could come from two or more sources, or from an investment or opportunity associated with versatility, communications, infotainment, or schooling, or from a brother, sister, or relative who is not your parent. Appreciate the wealth of having loving, supportive relatives in your life, if you are fortunate enough to have some.

SUN IN CANCER

(JUNE 21–JULY 22)

QUALITY *Cardinal* → | **ELEMENT** *Water* ◊

W hile highly sensitive in the way they behave toward others, Cancerians are usually most sensitive when it comes to their own feelings. They are more easily hurt than other signs, especially if their kindness is rejected or not reciprocated. Hurt a Cancer's feelings and they may sulk.

When you have to make a decision, you arrive at your conclusions slowly and deliberately. As a Cancer, you are guided by your feelings. Once your mind is made up, you seldom change it. Those you care about are sacred to you and you need your family and friends to have

those same devoted feelings toward you. You seldom make mistakes when you follow your own intuitions.

You enjoy nurturing people in general and especially children and those who cannot take care of themselves well. The past means a lot to you, and so entertaining family and friends on holidays and anniversaries is one of your favorite things. Such celebrations give you an excuse to serve home-cooked meals and to exchange thoughtful gifts. You like to reminisce about events that you experienced or that concern family, friends, acquaintances, and relatives of bygone generations. You hold older people in high esteem and also love to tell children about the past as a teaching experience, helping them to avoid the mistakes of youth. Souvenirs and mementos are a great delight. You cherish things that are linked with your early years.

In astrology, Cancer rules the home and is the nurturing caregiver. People like to visit you and your home or any place where you have made your "nest." Often, they have no other reason for calling than to bask in the warmth of your cheerfulness. You enjoy mainly indoor pastimes or ones that are close to home, especially preparing and serving food. You like to keep in touch with cultural progress by going to lectures and participating in community projects and group discussions. You care deeply about personal and family security. That is why you like to acquire property and possessions. Your aim is to increase the value of the things you acquire for the sake of future security. You are skilled at making your home base secure.

Perhaps at times you have been regarded as timid because you are shy, do not seek public recognition, and dislike aggression. Few realize how brave you can be in the defense of those under your protection.

Your persistence and a rare degree of emotional intelligence enable you to go through difficult experiences despite your aversion to physical and mental suffering. You gain in wisdom and in spiritual strength through these experiences and this knowledge enables you to aid or sympathize with others.

You know what it means to be caught unawares by circumstances without ready access to protective armor. Your good deeds are motivated by the wish to be saved and to save others from having to feel the pain that is inflicted by ignorant, uncaring, and hurtful people. Helping to keep others away from harm enables you to create a bright aura of peace and happiness around yourself.

Books and music can change your life. You like to read, but what you like even more is to have a library full of books and media of all forms that date back to childhood. Music has the same charm for you because you can spend many hours listening to, or playing, your favorite tunes. It does not take much effort on your part to become a skillful musician, because you feel the resonance of music as well as understand its rhythms.

While you find enjoyment in family, you are drawn to outsiders as well: You always do your best to keep on good terms with everyone. You tend toward practical idealism. For instance, you do not believe in razing a beautiful old building to make way for a new edifice, just for the sake of being modern. On the other hand, you would not spare expense in the building of a public recreation center, playground, assisted living facility, or hospital.

· · LOVE AND RELATIONSHIPS · ·

Cancers need to be with someone who loves them and is dependable. You need to be supported and loved unconditionally. You, in turn, need to nurture your partner and make them feel safe. Be on the lookout for a person who embodies these loving, gentle qualities.

If that kind of relationship is not attractive to you, be aware that you could be equating intensity, uncertainty, and even danger with passion and true love. You may be setting yourself up to avoid having a relationship that will last.

If you do not have a relationship but want one, be mindful that the problem could be related to issues of mothering and nurturing.

You may be looking for someone to take care of you or you may be repelled by anyone who needs to be taken care of in some way. Or it may be hard to find a partner who shares your views on children and child-rearing.

It is important that any relationship you are in makes you feel secure. When you are with your partner, you should feel at home and like you have no need to be anywhere else. You may be surprised at how your maternal feelings rise within you when you love someone.

Any problems you are experiencing with your love life are probably the result of childhood experiences. This could range from you and your partner coming from very different upbringings to serious traumas one or both of you suffered as children. Place your emphasis on the value of constructive living—of taking responsibility for who you are now and putting the past in its proper place. Even if your own childhood was extremely happy or sad, trying to apply experiences

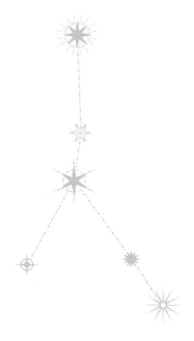

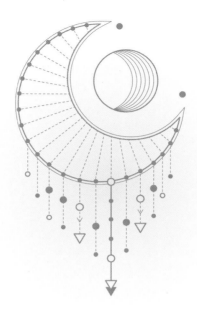

from your past without considering present conditions can create a great deal of stress for you and your partner. Learn from the past but live in the moment.

If you are not in a relationship and have been wondering what you can do to attract one, spend time making your home into the kind of secure nest where a great relationship can be born and grow. True love may come to you when you do not expect it, when you have the intention to feel that kind of love. A relationship may come to you through family or people you consider your family.

Not all people are capable of displaying their feelings as much as you would like them to. It would be a pity if shyness prevented you from meeting someone you would come to love passionately. Sometimes a slow fire burns the longest.

If you find that your partner or someone you are interested in does not want to do the work necessary to strengthen your relationship, be thankful that you found this out while there's still time to do something about it.

·· WORK AND CAREER ··

In your work situation, it is vital that you feel like you have found a home. You are sensitive to work that reminds you in some way of the work done by you or your family in the past. It is the Cancer way, not a sign of weakness or nepotism, if family and friends can help your job and career. You may also be able to work out of your home more easily than the other eleven signs.

Remember, examine, and learn from any work-related or career mistakes. It is not necessary to seek out all involved and make amends, though that might be a good thing to do. For your own wellness, it is most important that you come to terms with your past so that you can feel secure enough to move forward.

At some time in the past your efforts to gain career advancement were made from a position of desperation. You did not allow yourself the luxury of addressing your own needs. That way of thinking and acting is probably no longer appropriate. In fact, if you do not take the time to stop and think about what would really make you feel secure, you will put a roadblock in the way of any new career success.

Examine what you believe it would take to make you feel secure in your work and career. Then formulate a plan to bring that security into your life. You cannot get what you want until you know what you want. Once you are clear about what that is, security can be yours— and more quickly than you would think possible.

It is important that Cancers do not take any unnecessary risks. There are probably opportunities for career advancement all around you, but you must feel safe and protected to make the best use of them.

The main theme for you in career matters is actually the first rule of warfare: make your base secure. Your self-protective instincts are very good, and you may even prefer a job in security or defense. The establishment of security requires a shrewd approach to everything you do, and Cancer is known for being shrewd enough to deal with those in their charge. This shrewdness could help you do well in the world of finance, investment—especially venture capital incubation of start-up companies—as well as fundraising.

Working at home would enable you to spend more time with your family, which is exactly what you like to do. Not only would you be able to devote more attention to your support system, but you would also be able to examine your feelings about your home and family. Those feelings are key to your achieving the kind of exciting career you may have been waiting for.

Occupations that are favored include those that enable you to address the needs of families, such as caregiving, food, clothing, household items, real estate, medicine, and all things connected with younger people and children. You would do well with careers involving nurturing of people, animals, and even businesses and other projects struggling to survive their first few years.

· · WEALTH AND SUCCESS · ·

You might profit from the work and advice of your close family, people from your past, and long-term investments. Retirement planning is especially favored. Real estate, especially real estate you or your family intend to live on, is also a good investment, as are any and all improvements that you make to where you live. Whether you live in a cave or a castle, making it more comfortable, more beautiful, and safer will always appeal to you. Collecting original art or crafts will feed your soul.

Another manifestation of this trait is that you could find yourself placed in an important and powerful position by those you consider your family. Administering a family trust would be one manifestation of this talent. If you are lucky enough to feel that your coworkers or even your boss is like family to you, then watch that area of your life for help or increased good fortune.

Don't risk getting involved with anything that might make you feel too insecure. Gambling is not a favored way for Cancer natives to gain

WELLNESS AND MINDFULNESS FOR CANCER

CANCER knows how to give and nurture as well as how to understand and share feelings and be protective. Therefore, learning how to avoid bottling up their emotions, suffering in silence, or being overprotective are some of the most important mindfulness lessons for Cancer.

Make your home base secure and you will feel comfortable no matter where you go. Things that remind you of happier times, such as comfort food, photographs, and souvenirs, are essential parts of ensuring you stay mindful and grounded when your innate sensitivity threatens to overwhelm you.

wealth unless they learned how to do it as a business from a family member, especially when they were young.

There is benefit for you from staying in a safe position you know a lot about, rather than from moving on to something new. You should not distract or pressure yourself with the stress of moving too fast. It will prevent you from seeing the opportunities around you.

Previous good deeds and people from your past may reward you when least expected. People who you took care of or who took care of you may come back again to bring you true wealth. If you are having financial problems, try turning to your close family or chosen family for advice or help.

Awards and recognition are most likely to come from organizations connected with your home or your past, or ones that are concerned with families, products for the home, or family values. Enter any lotteries or contests with close friends and family.

If there are any children in your life, be nurturing and protect them financially. That should include showing them life skills, especially how to live on a budget and run a home. Sometimes being a little overprotective is called for. It is very important that you and your loved ones feel safe and protected because important events that may unfold for your benefit require that security to be able to manifest themselves.

If you take some time to investigate the past, you may be surprised to learn new and very interesting information about family members, both those still living and those who have passed over. You will be amazed how the issues of your grandparents might seem to have been miraculously transferred to the children in your life.

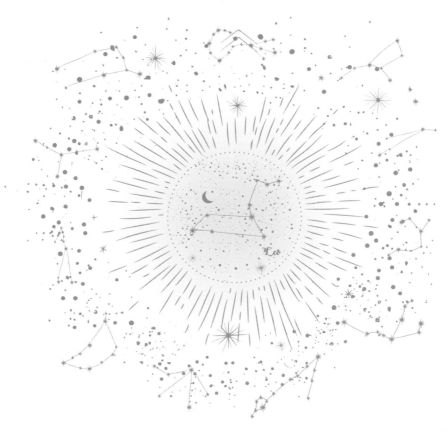

SUN IN LEO

(JULY 23–AUGUST 22)

QUALITY *Fixed* ◊ | **ELEMENT** *Fire* ♦

Your place in the world is to lead others and show them how things are done. But at times Leos must put on an act to get the job done. Leos find it very difficult to be a team player, because they feel it is their lot to lead. Leos need to remember that "one who would lead must follow all."

You have the dynamic ability to command obedience and you can do so without being harsh or dictatorial. You are at your best as a capable leader when you make tactful suggestions that let everyone feel included. You do this as well in routine occupations as in executive work.

Your personality usually reflects creative and extroverted qualities. At times when you are uncertain, however, you can see yourself as being shy, introspective, and rather inhibited. This skewed self-image is usually due to the self-centered attributes of Leo.

You like to dress well and have other people notice it. You are style conscious to some extent, but in astrology Leo is associated with creativity. Being fashion forward is fun for you. You like to indulge your creativity by putting together new or striking combinations or even designing your own clothing. For some garments you instinctively seek bright colors. Leo is ruled by the sun, and sunny colors, such as orange, gold, and bronze, will usually occupy important places in your wardrobe.

You like your home to be comfortable and then some—even luxurious. Leo the lion is king of the jungle, so make your home your castle. You derive great pride, an important part of being a Leo, from having a beautiful residence to which you can invite relatives and friends. Also, you like to visit others who know how to entertain guests on a lavish scale.

One of your seasonal pleasures is to garden, though you might not want to do the unglamorous parts like weeding. For indoor recreation, you enjoy movies and streaming videos, music, concerts, art exhibitions, and the theater. You are probably an enthusiastic and avid reader of world news. You keep in touch with a large circle of friends and your texts and emails are often quoted by others.

Although home is important for you, you also like to travel, but only in high style. It would be a rare Leo who turned down an invitation to travel if someone else offered to pay.

It is instinctive for you to be outgoing. You are willing to do favors for people you know well, as well as be gracious to those whom you meet for the first time, as if you were an ambassador.

Any place where you can be yourself, which includes using your innate acting ability to behave like a slightly different person when you travel, appeals to you.

Leos are generous with their time, money, and possessions. It is always satisfying for you to go on a useful errand or to be of service to anyone who needs help. You like to play with children and find pleasure in watching them, though you're more than willing to leave their care to someone else. You win their affection because you know how to enter their imaginary play world, and because you are a good teacher. You instruct by example rather than by rote, as befits a leader.

Instinctively you assume leadership at home, but you manage to give the impression that your mate is head of the family. Your mental scope is characterized by a good memory, knowledge gained through study and observation, the ability to benefit from past mistakes, a desire to improve your ideas, and the wish to think constructively about any subject. This wide range enables you to remember the significant incidents in your life and use them in instructional storytelling. You can make constructive use of past happenings in contemporary situations.

Your friendliness and warm feelings are genuine. You often use your sincerity, kindness, and humor to see who you are dealing with. If they react well, you know they are confident and polite. You can also use the same traits and your acting ability as a protective barrier against those who are sly, secretive, or inauthentic. You can size up those who are unreliable quickly and you know upon first impression who is worthy of your trust.

You enjoy being leisurely about keeping appointments. You mean to be prompt, but when you are late you see no reason for profuse apologies because you know that you are worth waiting for. However, you show your displeasure when you are kept waiting. Noble Leos believe that they are entitled to consideration for their convenience.

The present moment is of paramount importance to you. Although you show respect for the experiences of others, you do not care to indulge in their regrets. Your belief is that whatever is gone should be forgotten.

You like to do things that can be approved by others. Whether you receive the desired response from them or not, you keep trying on your own behalf until you achieve the ultimate fulfillment of your ideals.

· · LOVE AND RELATIONSHIPS · ·

The Leo nature is generous in showing love but also seriously craves affection. You would decide without hesitation to take love over wealth or fame. You can be deeply hurt when someone is indifferent to your devotion, because you are very loyal.

You are a romantic. And sometimes you just have to take a chance on the fact that it is possible to find true love. We have seen Leos happily married to other Leos, but marriage between two people with the same sign is rare for the other signs.

Leos enjoy all kinds of fun and creative endeavors. You might work on a project with a love interest, as you enjoy the mutual support. You might also attend creative classes together, visit museums, or go to concerts, comedy clubs, art galleries, movies, dance recitals, concerts, or the theater.

You have to make time in your schedule for amorous interludes. A relationship that allows you to experience a romantic thrill can strengthen with time and be very rewarding. A relationship where there is no more feeling of excitement is in danger of ending.

Relationships with children will also be favored for a Leo. If you do share in the raising of children, they will be a source of pride and joy.

Relationship problems may emerge from not making time for fun and romance, or poor results from investments and other calculated risks. There is also the possibility that children may be the problem, or your views on children may conflict, especially about the conditions necessary to bring a child into the world.

WELLNESS AND MINDFULNESS FOR LEO

LEO knows how to persevere and be respected by becoming a steady and focused creative force. They like to lead and be noticed. Therefore, staying mindful of the fact that true leadership is doing what is best for those they lead is one of the most important lessons for Leo.

Leo rules the heart, back, and spine. Dancing is perfect for keeping a Leo fit, happy, and looking like a star. The cat stretch yoga pose is helpful for strengthening the back and opens the heart chakra. Leos must remember they are spirits learning and growing.

But remember, children are a separate issue from your relationship. When you can admit that you do or do not feel that they are a great joy and a great responsibility that cannot be ignored, and you and your partner are in sync about this, then you will be on the path to a healthy relationship.

Having children is not for everyone. Having them because you are "supposed to" or to satisfy the wishes of relatives will create an almost overwhelming amount of hard work and health-damaging stress for a Leo. Bringing children into this world without being able to provide for them physically, emotionally, intellectually, and spiritually will challenge your relationship.

You will recognize your ideal partner because everyone's head will turn when they enter a room. For Leo, time together tends to be both romantic and dramatic. Your partner must treat you like royalty and everyone else should treat you both like celebrities.

Trouble in your relationships could also be caused by problems related to organization, responsibility, and leadership. If one or both of you is unwilling to act responsibly or if one or both of you wants to take a leadership role in your relationship, the result will be the same.

Be mindful that a successful relationship is not one in which everything is split down the middle. It is one where each person does what they do best in a spirit of service to the other person. If you find that there are many essential tasks that neither of you is good at, then you must both try your best to do them together.

· · WORK AND CAREER · ·

You can have tremendous success with work requiring creativity and inspired ideas. There are opportunities around you to be creative in any job. Though mental work is usually associated with a fertile imagination, you can also be quite clever in work requiring physical labor. Your creativity can be expressed in finding ways to do your work better or more efficiently.

Leo rules entertainment. A job in traditionally artistic fields like the visual arts, sculpture, music, dance, film, TV, writing, design, or fashion would be quite suitable for a Leo's temperament.

If you have ever thought of acting, a profession that is ruled by Leo, you should at least try auditioning for a part. Other jobs that may manifest themselves are the riskier side of investing, sports-related work, gaming of all kinds, and opportunities to display goods. You may also find yourself called on to do some public speaking.

Be mindful that it is very important for you to express your ability to innovate solutions to problems and make improvements to established rules. Whatever you do, you should produce work that is a reflection of your unique personality and purpose.

Producing this inspired work is like giving birth to a child. You are bringing into the world something that has never existed in just that form before. And like a child, whatever you create takes on a life of its own and needs you to let it go at some point.

If you find that there are those around you who resist your original ideas, you must use your Leo leadership and acting skills to convince them to let you give your ideas a try. This requires you to look at your involvement in a creative way.

Do not just accept that you and those around you know the best way to create or accomplish a goal. Try looking at your situation as if you have never seen it before or as if you were a child looking at it. Or bring in someone, maybe even a young person, and explain your problem to them.

If you are between jobs, do not waste time thinking that you have failed in some way. Use this time to look at your strengths and weaknesses and choose a job that allows you to do what you are best at. Do not settle for a job that won't challenge you to innovate or you will be plagued with a nagging dissatisfaction.

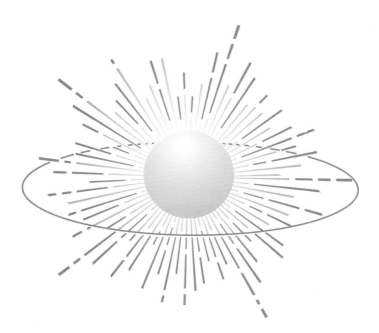

Your good fortune can best come to you through having fun, enjoying love and romance, and—you guessed it—being creative. If you can look at even your routine tasks as pleasurable, that attitude and energy will bring more wealth and success into your life.

The purpose of life is to be happy. Pleasure is a wonderful experience, and Leos would agree. It is the opposite of pain, another fact no one will deny. However, what most people do not realize is the many ways in which pain, other than physical pain, is actually a resistance to love.

The more a Leo learns how to run their life around what they enjoy, the better their life will be, as will the lives of those around them. You are not being selfish when you are enjoying yourself; you are fulfilling your divine purpose as a human being. If you do not allow yourself to enjoy pleasure, you can only be telling yourself that you would prefer to live with pain, and your powerful subconscious mind will help you find painful situations.

You stand to benefit tremendously from helping younger people or the child within you understand what life is all about. The best way to accomplish this would be through play, another Leo special skill. Teach children to think of success as a game and to just have fun with it. If it is taken too seriously, success becomes a target that always gets farther and farther away.

Role-playing is another form of acting. If you have been having problems with your resources, try acting out the part of you that wants to be wealthy and successful, and then play the part of you that does not. Both of those parts are in everyone.

You can profit from performing, producing, or sometimes even just watching performances, both live and recorded. A brilliant idea could come to you as you are playing or watching. In this information age, ideas are currency. Your creative explorations can lead you to many marketable ideas. If you have been working on a project that could pay you royalties, that is a great idea. Leo's symbol is the lion, king of the jungle, and royalties are so named because they enable one to live like a king or queen.

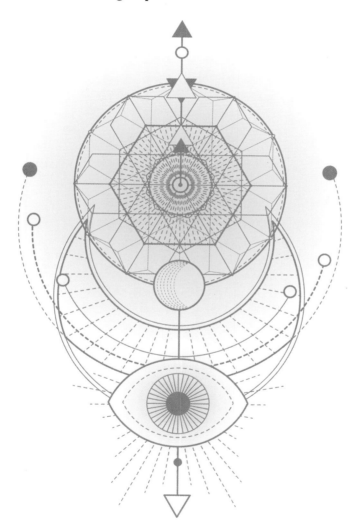

SUN IN VIRGO

(AUGUST 23–SEPTEMBER 22)

QUALITY *Mutable* ≈ | **ELEMENT** *Earth* 🜨

At the heart of the typical Virgo is the hardest and most skilled worker you've ever met—ready, willing, and able to help anyone they deem worthy of Virgo-style, aim-for-perfection service. And yet a surprising number of Virgos would often rather do nothing than do the wrong thing or do something less than perfectly, which often leads others to see them as procrastinators, rather than perfectionists.

As a Virgo, you value your personal safety and seldom take unnecessary risks. You are concerned with the exactness and artistry of the work you do, pouring all of your effort into each task. You train yourself to use your time efficiently to achieve the best results.

You demonstrate your love of perfection in your apparel and your manners. What you wear is well made and you usually look well groomed. You dislike disorder, grime, and uncouth behavior, unless this is part of a particular look you are going for. This instinct for orderliness causes you to point out others' mistakes, a trait that leads to Virgos being known as the critics of the zodiac.

You try to express your observations humorously, and your stories about the mistakes of others can keep a roomful of people laughing. You do not mean to be malicious but your gift of humor and your tendency to criticize can sometimes merge.

Your manual dexterity and mental versatility qualify you to do well in such vocations as a teacher, designer, technician, critic, musician, statistician, chef, or healer.

Most Virgos prefer to be alone rather than in the midst of a noisy crowd. However, you are willing to give time and service to civic, social, and spiritual organizations that work unobtrusively for the welfare of the public.

You are a great believer in preventive measures once you decide that they will work and fit into your daily routine. From your viewpoint, mistakes should be avoided. As a perfectionist, you know all too well that there would have been less loss and stress if the blunders had not occurred.

You do not have trouble making up your mind about what is right and wrong. You feel certain of the proper procedure even though your actions are sometimes limited by your aforementioned propensity to do nothing rather than do something halfway.

Your resourcefulness seldom falters, even in the face of restrictions. You appear indecisive now and then, but your decisions about the most effective best practices rarely have to be revised. You will often change your schedule to please others, not because you lack confidence in your own accuracy or timing.

Wasteful habits are abhorrent to you. Buying things for which you cannot pay promptly is against your code, and you do not like owing people money. Though you are much less hard on other people than you are on yourself, you do expect others to be equally prudent.

You have exacting taste in music and reading matter. Your quest for perfection is reflected in everything you appreciate about the work of others in every endeavor.

The application of your knowledge and excellent taste enables you to serve as a specialist or consultant. Even acknowledged experts who come to know you will seek and defer to your opinion because your suggestions are clear and your advice remarkably unbiased.

You realize how important proper food is to the human body. Preparing and serving healthy meals is instinctive with you because you have a natural comprehension of suitable foods and cooking technique. The Virgo skill at breaking down a task to its component parts so as to analyze the best way to accomplish it mirrors our body's

ability to break down the food we eat into the nutrients we need to stay alive.

You need to associate with people who are capable and considerate. You can get along well with a lot of different people provided they are pleasant enough so that you feel responsive to them. You are realistic and practical, though the Virgo tendency to see every detail of a situation but not the big picture can make your unique practicality seem rather impractical.

· · LOVE AND RELATIONSHIPS · ·

It is important that you, your partner, or both of you love your work or at least feel you are providing a useful service. If you do not, avoid bringing work into your relationship because your complaints may produce problems. Some Virgos might even try working with or for the benefit of their partner. Do this only if your circumstances and your temperament are up to the task.

If you are not in a relationship now and want to be, one might come to you either through your coworkers or volunteer work that you do. Any important relationships that come into your life will have an element of service to them, either you helping your new friends or they, you.

As a Virgo, you view health in mind, body, and spirit as the ultimate blessing. If you lack that health it is important that your partner understands your health challenges and wants to do all they can to help you cope.

Virgos like to be useful and of service to their partners, but be careful not to force your help on anyone. Do not waste your time with people whose fears drive them away from people who need help, if that is your situation, or with people who do not want to be helped by another person. We are all healing from the challenges we have lived through and can share our experience with those who want our help.

Sometimes you and your partner may go through a stage of becoming more aware of each other's habits, especially relating to health, cleanliness, neatness, eating, sleeping, and working. Be mindful that little habits that become known too soon might prove the undoing of a relationship. Once you have gotten to know, like, and respect each other, these little habits are far more likely to be tolerated.

Problems with partners may also be a result of your attitude toward criticism. If you do not have a partner and want one, do not criticize yourself. You may be too self-critical and will therefore not believe someone who says that they like you. It is also possible that you are sensitive if potential partners seem to be overly critical or unable to handle criticism.

Fear of criticism can lead you to search out a younger, simpler, less successful, or less educated person who would be less likely to criticize you. This may work out but could prove disastrous later if your partner learns how to criticize from you.

Criticism is a tool; like a hammer, it can be constructive and used to build, or destructive and used to destroy. Being critical can become a habit, so look inside yourself to see whether this is true for you or your partner. If it is, stop it as best you can. If you become aware that you are overly picky or anxious or being a perfectionist, remind yourself how many of your past worries were for nothing and that you can handle anything.

Be mindful that a lot of seemingly trivial issues about health, food, cleanliness, being of service, and work have an important impact on your relationships. Worrying or being attached to a particular outcome will not help. Remember that peace begins when your expectations end.

If you use your critical ability with a conscious intent to help your partner or a potential partner, keep in mind that the justness of your criticism must be tempered with the mercy of your mutual love; this will help you to build a loving relationship on the firmest of foundations.

WELLNESS AND MINDFULNESS FOR VIRGO

VIRGO knows how to be of service and how to review, fix, edit, and adjust to circumstances. Virgos can worry about little things and be overly critical and analytical. Therefore, learning how to be mindful of their perfectionism is one of the most important lessons for Virgo.

Virgos thrive on organization and order. They are uncompromising, tend to be fussy, and enjoy precision. Therefore, they would benefit from a cursory (not perfect) cleaning and clearing of their space as an empowering, healing, comforting self-care protocol.

· · WORK AND CAREER · ·

Crucial to the advancement of a Virgo's career is your willingness to do the often boring, routine, and even menial tasks. Expecting someone else to take care of them will only delay what you desire. Get down to work and get moving, even if it seems pointless.

It is good for you to be recognized for what you can do, not for what you say. Show those in a position to help you that you are not afraid to work hard. A Virgo is usually able to make something out of any job. It is not always the line of work, but how hard you work that counts.

Be mindful, however, that sometimes working too hard can be just as bad as not working hard enough. In your attempt to balance your career goals with your physical and mental health, you must pay attention to health habits, rest and relaxation, and especially proper nutrition. Those who ignore even one of these often come to regret it.

Many people are willing to avoid taking proper care of their body's needs in their pursuit of a career and wear this as a badge of honor.

However, when your hard work pays off, you will want to be as healthy as you can be to enjoy it to the fullest.

It is best for Virgos to work hard at what they do but not focus on their overall career. Big career plans and ideas for expansion are not as important as taking care of the details. Every little job or project that you are involved with can become important to your overall career, but you often cannot tell which ones. So it's best to give your attention to each and every one of the seemingly small matters.

Even pleasantries and minor rules and regulations that might ordinarily be ignored can become very important in your daily work routine. Pay close attention to precise meanings of words and the interpretation of policies. Take nothing for granted.

There is nothing to be ashamed of in taking care of the little things that make the big things work. Attend to those small but critical

details and, as you do so, realize that the importance of things does not always match their size. Attending to details can often lead to worry because there seem to be almost too many details to deal with. Remember how many times your worries have been for nothing. Many of your present worries are most likely for nothing now.

Virgos excel at work requiring their ability to break things down and analyze them. Health care, chemistry, pharmacology, engineering, and architectural design, especially the planning and details of these fields, come to mind immediately, but there are many other careers where your precise manner and keen eye will benefit you. Quality control is especially good. All arts that require masterful hand-eye coordination lend themselves to Virgo precision and attention to detail.

· · WEALTH AND SUCCESS · ·

The biggest obstacle to a Virgo obtaining, keeping, and growing their wealth is their tendency to worry about just how things are going to turn out, also known as their attachment to outcomes.

We each bring into our lives experiences that teach us the lessons we would like to learn. It is up to you to decide what you can learn from your present experience. If you spend time worrying about how things are going to turn out or thinking about what you do not have, you are wasting time that could be spent helping you increase your wealth and standing.

How you are able to deal with life on a mental and emotional level determines how things will manifest in your life. If you remember that you are strong and can handle anything life brings you, you will bring into your life experiences that prove this is true.

The easiest way for a Virgo to make money is simply to earn it. Everything you get probably will be the result of hard work, and in your heart of hearts, this is the way you like it to be.

Virgos like to be paid when a job is completed. If they do get money advanced to them, they have to be very careful with it. For some reason, this situation is like having a pebble in your shoe. There's something about being paid in full for work that has not yet been done that does not sit well with the legendary Virgo work ethic.

Virgos are masters at "getting their karma" quickly. If you have doubts about your abilities, life will bring you challenges. Sometimes it takes overcoming fairly unpleasant circumstances to convince you of your intelligence, strength, and endurance. Once this is done, your powerful subconscious mind will allow you to experience situations that increase your wealth and success.

Be mindful to treat your health like the ultimate wealth that it is. Without it, no amount of wealth and success is going to be as useful to you. Maintain a positive, confident, and grateful attitude, and do not let what you lack prevent you from enjoying what you have.

Worries about wealth and success will actually stop the flow of both things to you. You really do have all that you need to get what you want.

It is a matter of accepting your situation, starting from where you find yourself, and taking small but practical steps toward your goal.

Worry is based on our attachment to wanting to know how things will turn out. The way to balance worry is to first acknowledge that it is based on our natural desire to avoid pain. Worry is like a well-meaning friend who keeps picking everything apart to try to make it better, yet this ends up as a pile of picked-apart pieces of a whole that does not work anymore. Let worry have its say and thank it for its trouble. In this way, worries are allowed to serve their legitimate purpose and you will not feel bad every time you notice you are worrying.

Contests related to food, health, and hygiene would be of particular benefit to Virgos, though many of them are reluctant to enter contests with no skill involved. Volunteer work would help you feel undeniably useful and it would help you calm your mind, the key to a Virgo seeing the path to wealth and success. Try to be in the moment by practicing meditation, breathing, and mindfulness.

SUN IN LIBRA

(SEPTEMBER 23–OCTOBER 22)

QUALITY *Cardinal* → | **ELEMENT** *Air* ≒

Other people may misinterpret a Libra's desire for peace, harmony, and beauty as an elitist attitude or snobbishness, but it is not. For many Libras, crude behavior is as much of an affront as a tirade of insults. A Libra may give the impression of being a pushover because of a seeming unwillingness to argue, but if their debate opponent is obviously impervious to logic, the Libra will leave the argument. Under the right set of circumstances, however, even the most unassuming Libra can stand up for themselves.

Even a Libra's most caring actions are the orderly reflection of their mental processes. You think things through from cause to effect as if you are on the outside looking in. This distanced overview makes it possible for you to avoid becoming flustered. You are able to see both sides of a question, and many of your friends depend on you to serve as a referee when they become involved in a dispute. This skill can be used successfully in the legal professions, education, and social work. The same alertness gives you great discernment in all forms of art and design. It makes you a keen judge of people, too.

You like your home to be attractive, filled with comfortable and harmonious furnishings. You need leisure time every day to pursue matters of greater interest to you than day-to-day tasks. Your most vital need is an all-embracing interest in a worthwhile cause.

You possess a great sense of humor. This manifests itself in a talent for sociability and party planning. You find relaxation in both quiet and active recreation because you can become skillful at either. You like to explore out-of-the-way places and then come home to tell your friends about your excursions.

Others listen to what Libras have to say without interrupting because you have a knack for describing your adventures or thoughts in an alluring way. Your code of ethics is governed by your logical ideals and sense of justice. You believe everyone is entitled to the privileges of "life, liberty, and the pursuit of happiness." You seek the good things in life for yourself, and you feel that others should have the right to attain those same goals.

You can appear quite serene even when you are facing Libra's biggest challenge: indecision. Deciding requires information, but it is almost impossible to get all the information that you want. Libras sometimes decide not to decide just yet, believing that they will soon have enough to go on, but this usually does not work out. Learning how to add the quiet voice of their intuition to their decision-making mix is a lifelong study for Libras, but it is a worthwhile pursuit.

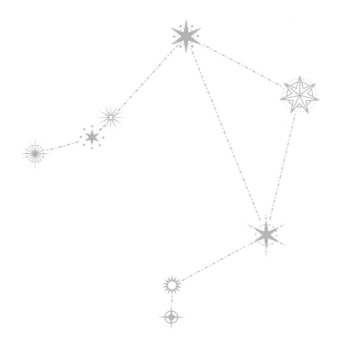

Even if a Libra feels upset, they do not let their annoyance become apparent because they dislike unnecessary turmoil. Libras often succeed in deflecting tension by appearing to be impervious to conflict. Anyone who has a short temper usually becomes reconciled to keeping it under control around Libras because Libras make it apparent that they will not participate in pointless arguments. You find it easier to arbitrate than to quarrel but, surprisingly, you can be quite aggressive in the defense of truth and fairness.

You are devoted to your loved ones, but not in a possessive or jealous way. Your emotional balance extends to your relationships with business associates and friends. You let others do as they please and expect them to refrain from interfering with you.

When shopping for clothes and accessories, you look for balance of color, harmony in design, quality, texture, and continued usefulness. Appreciation of beauty is part of your nature. Most Libras prefer to wear clothes that are in style and of superior quality.

Your poise, good humor, keen appreciation, and esthetic tastes prove helpful in keeping all personal relationships idealistic and harmonious. You feel inspired when you are associated with anyone who participates in the arts or who is a recognized expert in their field. You go out of your way to boost anyone who is talented and kind.

You can succeed in your career objectives because you have the qualities of mind of patience, courage, and persistence. When you are asked to do anything with which you are not familiar, you prefer to take the time to learn and, if time permits, to master the technique. You make sure that you understand any subject thoroughly before you label yourself a professional.

You take pride in what you do. You want to be praised and admired for your accomplishments, and you become annoyed if you are not acknowledged. This annoyance can prey on your good humor, so when you find yourself being aggressive or sarcastic, examine whether you are allowing a slight to spoil your good time.

Libras are inclined to draw their circle of family and friends into their efforts. Through your endeavors and influence, many of your friends and relatives will gain a solidarity of purpose.

Nevertheless, you always keep a professional distance, just in case someone you are trying to help does not measure up to the standards of the person you have connected them with. You believe in maintaining your own individuality and are satisfied to let others adhere to theirs. You know how to blend harmoniously with others. When you give a promise, you carry it out to the best of your ability.

If you can avoid becoming too self-assured or too complacent, you can accomplish great things. You can be helpful and considerate, but there are times when your sense of equanimity causes you to assume that your way is best. In cases where you can't do things your way, you may refrain from acting so you don't waste valuable time and potential opportunities that could work toward your benefit.

· · LOVE AND RELATIONSHIPS · ·

Relationships, both romantic and committed partnerships of all kinds, are naturally very important to a Libra, one of the two signs ruled by the planet of love, Venus.

You'll know you have found your soul mate when neither of you wants to change the other, only to enjoy life together and help each other fulfill your individual dreams. This does not happen on the first date, but the essentials of mutual attraction, trust, respect, and friendship may be felt. Wishful thinking can easily confuse the issue, so relax, seek to see things as clearly as possible, and be yourself.

Any trouble in a relationship will come from one or both of you not fulfilling your obligations with honesty and a generous heart. You or your partner may have learned from others that this unequal and disappointing behavior was the appropriate way to act in a relationship. Troubled marriages and divorce can affect the participants and especially their children a lot more than anyone would care to admit, especially if they are Libras.

Any problems you are having in finding or maintaining a relationship can probably be traced back to your inability to see that you have a tendency to first idealize your partner and then to feel let down when you realize that your partner is a human being. In order for you to bring the most healthy, balanced kind of relationship into your life, make the necessary changes in your attitude toward your partner. There are no perfect people or perfect partnerships. Compromise comes naturally to Libras when they let go of wanting to be judged as faultless.

The trick in both romantic and business relationships for Libras is to avoid living your life through the needs and demands of your partner. Living that way can be the easy way out for a Libra because you will not have to acknowledge your own needs and take action to make your dreams come true. A relationship based on satisfying the needs of only one of the people involved is doomed to failure.

If you are blindly devoting yourself to finding an ideal person, it will cause you to miss opportunities to meet truly wonderful people. Like you, they are not as good as they are going to be one day, but they have potential. If you insist that they be a predefined level of rich, charming, good-looking, or any one of a dozen other conditions, you must face the fact that you may not be the one that such a perfect person would be interested in. If you are more realistic in your expectations, you are more likely to be attractive to a realistic person who would be good for you.

WELLNESS AND MINDFULNESS FOR LIBRA

LIBRAS know how to be fair in relationships and will work for justice. They can be diplomatic as well as surprisingly aggressive. Therefore, learning how to attain a balanced, harmonious approach to life is one of the most important mindfulness lessons for Libra.

Sitting erect, cross-legged with hands placed on knees—in yoga this is the "mudra" position—deepens the experience of meditation that is calming for the mind. Connecting breaths with an open and beautiful feeling helps a Libra stay balanced.

· · WORK AND CAREER · ·

It would be especially beneficial for you to work in any profession where your success depends on your ability to interact well with others—to be a team player. A group effort is actually the best way for you to advance your individual interests.

Your ability to size up a situation can help you do well as an attorney, a counselor, or a judge, but also as a professional buyer, purchasing agent, appraiser, or salesperson. Working in the worlds of fashion, design, or interior decoration would provide you with much success and pleasure. A job involving law enforcement or the law, especially contracts, would be a good use of your ability to work with others. Whatever job you are in, be the one who seeks harmony and beauty and to form partnerships, even with competitors.

Jobs that would also be a good fit with the Libra temperament could involve working with the public, publicity, negotiations, and working in the support industries that service weddings and parties. If possible, your work should have you as an equal part of a team.

You can advance your career more if you work in a partnership with a clear understanding of your goals and respective roles. Pay attention to the obligations you have at work. Fulfill your part of all agreements. Find a way to work with others without feeling that you have to give up your unique personality.

If you are having problems at work, look at how your actions could be interpreted. Think more before you act on your goals and take a minute to consider others' feelings. You may be surprised what this exercise reveals. If you cannot get over impatience with the pace of others or with the speed of your advancement, then try to hide it.

Whether you are looking for a new job or trying to do your best where you are, make a special effort to be mindful when you're discussing options with the various members of your team. Some of them may not be as comfortable as you are in stating their opinions. For them to act so forcefully would require them to be either egotistically sure of their opinion or angry enough not to care what you thought. Consider that this may be how they think you feel toward them.

If someone in a position to do you some good is confused by your actions, then you must help them see that you do not want their job . . . even if you might!

· · WEALTH AND SUCCESS · ·

Libras are often more successful if they join forces with one or more partners so as to benefit from two sets of connections, two chances to get lucky, and two people to help make decisions.

Even if you feel the need to develop your self-reliance, you will never be able to live the ideal Libra life in a world without other people. Your challenge is to be strong enough not to lose your individuality even though you have to be with another person to accumulate the wealth and success you have worked for. You will find that it will benefit you to keep the advice and generosity of others in mind.

You are always trying to balance the scales of justice and may sometimes have to be more aggressive to receive compensation that has been owed you for a while. Research contracts thoroughly before you sign them. Do not settle just to keep the peace.

Libras can best benefit from arrangements where everything is spelled out in writing. Some people will push back, but just inform them that contracts have existed for thousands of years so that people can be clear about what is expected of them. It is also a good idea, when necessary, to remind all who have yet to fulfill their commitments to you that they should always follow up on deals and agreements in a mindful way.

Publicity and coming before the public in all matters are also favored. If you are called on to speak in public or deal with the public, you will do very well. Other people may want to help you to further their own cause, or they could be acting like agents operating on your behalf, or you may benefit from representing someone else.

Libras are good at commitment, so partnerships are favored financially. If you are married, celebrate your relationship and your success. You could also go into business together.

Prizes and contests with the theme of partnership, publicity, diplomacy, harmony, and balance will be very good for you. Also, you could win recognition or awards given for art, design, and beautification.

SUN SIGNS | SUN IN LIBRA |

SUN IN SCORPIO

(OCTOBER 23–NOVEMBER 21)

QUALITY *Fixed* ◊ | **ELEMENT** *Water* ◊

There are actually two symbols for the sign of Scorpio. The most familiar is the scorpion, but the eagle sitting on a cactus eating a rattlesnake, which happens to be on the flag of Mexico, embodies Scorpio's rulership of extremes, of the highest and the lowest, day and night, and life and death. Scorpio is the sign associated with both sex for pleasure and reproduction, and our bodies' waste eliminative functions.

Scorpios emulate both the loftiness of the eagle and the sharp sting of the rattlesnake and scorpion. Though they are not known for it, Scorpios actually like to help people they feel are worthy and to have them realize they can depend on Scorpio in an emergency. But Scorpios cannot tolerate impositions from those they do not feel close to.

When anyone tries to take advantage of you, you can become vindictive and bitter until you feel that the law of karma has prevailed. Undeveloped Scorpios have a tendency to use their intimate understanding of human motivations for vengeance and also for ruthless manipulation of people to attain selfish goals.

Most Scorpios would never think of lowering themselves that way. The sign of Scorpio rules the concept of being misunderstood, and so there are many stereotypes about people born with the sun in Scorpio that are simply not true, a result of misinterpretation of Scorpio's ways and passions.

For example, an important but not well-known Scorpio trait is that the welfare of your family and friends means a great deal to you. You might deprive yourself of comforts and conveniences so that those you

MINDFUL ASTROLOGY

love will not be missing out. You prefer to keep your good deeds out of the limelight, a main reason these Scorpio traits aren't widely known.

While Scorpios are constantly trying to uncover the secrets of others, they guard their own privacy with almost manic intensity. You pursue the same code of secrecy in your opinions about people. When you cannot say anything good about a person, you do not say anything unless it is just the right time and your words could produce a useful result.

You do not proclaim your feelings from the rooftops. This reserved and dignified attitude brings you genuine respect from those who do not misinterpret it as an indication you are judging them. When you do share your words, they carry weight.

It is easy to confide in you because those who trust you with facts or valuables know that you will not betray them unless and until they betray you. If betrayal occurs, you will have your revenge, even if it takes a long time before you achieve it. A Scorpio must have coined the phrase "Revenge is a meal best served cold."

You are a natural-born custodian of other people's property and financial security as well as your own because you have high standards. You have the ability to impress others with your integrity and with your capacity to serve any cause tirelessly. You can be successful in an occupation that values focus and determination. As a technician, analyst, or efficiency expert, you could develop a distinguished record.

You have no patience with those who try to get something for nothing. You try to accomplish adequate results for the compensation you receive because you want to retain and increase your reputation for excellence and dependability.

You prefer to gather knowledge and wisdom through personal experience and real-life stories recounted by people you respect. You are skeptical about other information until you verify it personally. You do not accept superficial explanations—or superficial anything, for that matter.

The person who aspires to be your friend must be able to convince you using provable facts, rather than attempts to deceive or flatter you. It is the truth that you desire and you usually obtain it because you insist on accuracy. With Scorpios, things are simple—good or bad, yes or no, black or white.

The clothing you wear is usually extremely well made but not covered in designer logos, and it is selected to give you a dignified yet alluring appearance. Also, your accessories are not flashy; at home, you store them using a favorite method to keep them neat and orderly.

You like to be prompt for appointments, and to keep your budget so well balanced that you know specifically at any time the total amount of your income and expenditures. Your realistic attitude guards you against the unpleasant experiences you envision so easily. You are not affected by pleading or coaxing, and you would prefer to suffer any consequence rather than show weakness.

You are the best detective of all the zodiac signs. Your exemplary intuitive powers and situational awareness keep you from being fooled, including by your own false impressions.

Your tendency is to be suspicious toward people who give the slightest impression of being dishonest, weak, or unreliable. You cannot forgive or forget a wrong action, especially a deliberate one. You brood deeply, like a smoldering volcano, about real or perceived grievances. When you feel sufficiently exasperated, your anger can erupt and cause serious damage.

You have high regard for persistence. You like to give credit to those who conquer obstacles and are sincere. You also appreciate those who prove to you that they have self-control. You like to help people who have respect for your judgment and who follow your advice in straightening out difficulties, but you have no pity for those who ignore your words and suffer for it.

You are willing to fight for your rights, but covertly, though you are prepared to be belligerent when you see a defenseless person being mistreated. You are ready, to the best of your Scorpionic ability, to see through all lies and self-deceptions, to counsel and help those who are unhappy and discouraged.

You are capable of being a powerful executive and yet you can also be a competent associate. Often you have to prove your ability to do good work because much is expected of you. You can achieve remarkable results in direct proportion to your passion.

Scorpio is the sign associated with the words *sex, power*, and *magic*, so it should come as no surprise that this sign is perceived as sexy, powerful, and able to work what often appear to be miracles of transformation.

If you are involved with children, it is a good idea to remind yourself about your duty to protect them from seeing, hearing, and experiencing things beyond their years. Scorpios have a tendency to want to protect children from being overwhelmed by the more sordid aspects of adult life by exposing them to stories of it when they are too young to truly benefit.

Be aware that the children in your life could be holding some secrets from you. Most are probably the innocent secrets of childhood. Make sure that they know you are interested in them and that you will believe what they tell you. It is important that they know you are on their side. If not, they may believe someone else has their best interests at heart when, in fact, they do not.

· · LOVE AND RELATIONSHIPS · ·

You expect passion and intensity in your relationships—you don't go for half measures. Although your life may sometimes feel like a romance novel, this is as it should be. Relationships that you thought were over and done with may sometimes resurrect themselves. But a relationship that has been built on anything other than honesty will end. The use and exchange of power, especially on a sexual level, can either make or break your relationships.

Do not reveal secrets—be mysterious. You may discover that people have been telling you half-truths. Few people are as honest as a Scorpio, so give them a break. You are a great detective, and if you suspect someone of this, it would be easy for you to investigate. What you do with what you find out will be determined by your mood.

Your relationships can have an element of sexual tension, mystery, magic, and possibly compulsion. If a Scorpio's relationship has lost its spark, it must be rekindled immediately, or it will surely die. Begin a slow, patient, and loving dialogue about how things have gotten to this point and how you are going to transform your relationship. You will have to use all of your detective skills to keep the transformation moving along, but you can do it.

It will be very hard for you to resist giving yourself completely to a new love, but you should wait until you have proven your love to each other first. The reason people have sex before they are truly in love is because there is no training in what love really is.

Scorpio rules sex, but a Scorpio can be so passionate about the subject that they abstain from it for a time, especially before a marriage. A person who loves you for yourself should be understanding about any decisions you make, especially about something as important as sex. All too often, the sexual urge is not seen as just that, an urge. Blindly following our primal urges can only lead to disaster.

Many people equate attractiveness with the amount of overwhelming desire a person inspires. This is all well and good at the beginning of a relationship, but it would be orders of magnitude better if it existed along with mutual respect and genuine caring. Scorpio's passion extends to wanting to experience extremes of everything. Growing old together should be viewed as a privilege to be desired.

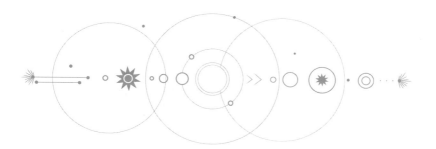

People often rush into a sexual relationship. This is not only physically dangerous, but unplanned pregnancy can destroy one's dreams and is often the result of a desire for approval.

A Scorpio who has experienced trauma can be identified by their surprising need for the approval of others. Feeling empty inside can also be a motivation for rushing into sex. When a Scorpio feels empty, they are willing to settle for any experience that feels important.

For a change, choose a partner you like and who is willing to wait a while before moving to the physical stage. This is not an exercise in self-denial; it is a way to increase your personal power.

When you find that person, a wonderful time in your life is at hand. Resisting your sexual urges is not easy for a Scorpio, but it clarifies whether you are in love or just in lust. You will know it is real when you actually want to reveal to your partner some (not all) of your secrets.

· · WORK AND CAREER · ·

Power, control, and secrecy are all important to a Scorpio. Keep secrets and do not volunteer information, even about the most trivial of things. Pretend that you are on a secret mission. When the time is right, you will be part of a major change for the better. When that happens, you will be able to enjoy your new and successful career move with anyone and everyone.

Scorpios may decide to end a job or an aspect of their career that is obviously not working for them. If this describes you, cut your losses and move on with confidence; the change will probably do you good. The sign of Scorpio rules both transformation and resurrection.

The necessity for secrecy may cause you to act like you know something others do not, and they may sometimes misunderstand. However, do not reveal secrets until you are sure, even to those you are positive will support you. The ability to keep knowledge away from

WELLNESS AND MINDFULNESS FOR SCORPIO

SCORPIOS know how to understand what motivates them and what makes others tick. They are devoted to exploring life at its extreme boundaries. Therefore, learning how to function well with less passionate people is one of the most important mindfulness lessons for Scorpio.

Aromatherapy would be very appealing for Scorpio. The enticing scent of wisteria, anise, or tuberose will suit their sexy natures, help them appreciate their mystical powers, and aid in healing past energetic traumas and hurtful boundary violations.

those not ready to hear it is as important as gaining the knowledge yourself. This is one of the secrets of making things happen.

Scorpios must try to avoid the temptation to manipulate people in the belief that the end justifies the means. This may prevent your dream from coming true. However, with a little forethought, this potential impediment is easily avoided, and the energy can be used instead to convince those who need convincing, a Scorpio strength.

If you have been thinking about making changes in your work situation or career, remember that Scorpio is a sign of extremes, so be prepared for change, but often it does not arise from an expected place.

Also, if you are thinking about a career change, drop a subtle, deniable hint to your most-trusted associates. If they are enthusiastic, you can tell them more. If they offer you their help, take it. Every successful person has received help from outside sources at one time or another, and there is no reason to let foolish pride stand in the way of a new career.

Learn how to use other people's money and resources to your advantage, either as a job or career in estate management, banking, or investment advising. It could be time for you to ask for more responsibility in your job, including handling other people's resources or money. If your request is granted, you must treat it as a sacred trust.

Whether you work with money or not, it is crucial that you resist any and all enticements to use your power for your own gain. It would also be a good idea to periodically use your spectacular detective abilities to make sure that your colleagues are being completely honest and not setting you up to take the fall for their nefarious activities.

At times, long-gone career plans will come back, but usually not the way you thought they would. If you are between jobs, consider doing a type of work that you have not done for a long time.

Work with a Scorpio flavor includes renovations, asset management, recycling, estate planning, detective work, the "mantic" arts (astrology, tarot, magic, and the like), banking, acting as an agent, and anything involved with sexuality.

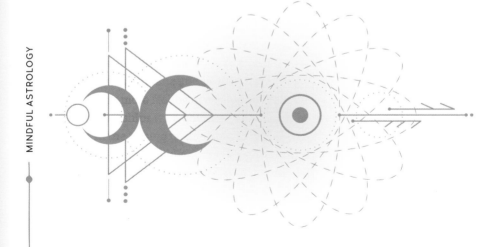

·· WEALTH AND SUCCESS ··

As a Scorpio, you could increase your wealth by using and managing other people's resources in addition to your own. If you do, it is important that you consistently appear to be managing them honestly, as well as successfully. Scorpio's rulership of the concept of misunderstanding can easily cause trouble when other people's money is involved.

Don't be surprised if you are able to make opportunities appear and obstacles disappear as if by magic. Scorpios really are very powerful and can influence others. You have the inclination and the ability to transform your resources profoundly, investing in one way and then making a major move to a whole other market segment, industry, or investment product. It will take thorough research, absolute secrecy, and a healthy suspicion of other people, but it can be done.

As a Scorpio, you will be open to seeing when obsolete investments of time, money, and other resources can come back to profitable life. You may find that something you once tried and failed at could be the perfect thing to profit from. Check your records and see what you can rework and resurrect profitably.

Once you know what to do, it would be better to use mostly other people's resources. You may have friends or family help you with a loan, grant, or early inheritance. If not, then investigate obtaining financial assistance from the many institutions, both governmental and private, that exist for just this purpose. Do this in secret.

A financial grant or loan would give you the freedom to devote yourself full time to the realization of your dreams for wealth and success. Scorpios can present themselves as the kind of people who can be trusted with other people's resources. You can gain financial wisdom from your efforts to obtain and pay back your loans. Once you have gotten your new enterprise going, you may find yourself guiding the wise use of other people's money as an advisor.

The quiet, intense Scorpio can sometimes seem open to a get-rich-quick scheme. As Scorpios know better than most, if it looks too good to be true, it probably is. Check into the secret details of any financial dealings you are thinking of becoming involved with. Do not volunteer information unless you have to. If someone confides in you, keeping their confidence will pay off in the long run.

You would have the best luck at contests where your ability to discover or even just plain guess secrets wins you a prize. You should be able to win something if it has a magical, mystical, or detective theme. You could also have success at receiving gifts from others in the form of grants, scholarships, and inheritances.

Take time to think about planning your estate or setting up a trust fund. It is very important to make sure that your desires are carried out after you pass. This is good advice for everyone, but especially for Scorpios, the sign that rules legacies and inheritances.

SUN IN SAGITTARIUS

(NOVEMBER 22–DECEMBER 21)

QUALITY *Mutable* ≈ | **ELEMENT** *Fire* 🔥

S agittarians are the sign most prone to tell you their truth even if you have not asked for it and even if it is not in their best interest. Scorpio knows the truth but prefers to keep it secret. Sagittarius also knows the truth, but has to say it or else they feel like they are lying.

Sagittarians are vivacious, enthusiastic, and able to adapt to changing circumstances. You rarely feel sorry for yourself. You are too conscious of your qualifications and life experience to appear hesitant or timid.

Sagittarians are dedicated to expanding their understanding of the way the world works. The sign is best known for doing this through actual long-distance travel, but also through travel in their mind via philosophy and learning.

Even after a prolonged tussle with adversity, you find that your optimism and sense of humor usually bounce back. You seldom permit yourself to become depressed. You prefer to associate with people who possess your bravery and frankness, rather than those who are too inhibited. When you want to make a statement, you get to the point quickly and honestly—sometimes too honestly.

You have no patience with long, drawn-out arguments. You save time by being logical and lucid, and you expect others to be just as succinct when they want to keep your interest. You crave a certain amount of daily alone time, preferably out in nature, because you never become bored with your own thoughts. You like to keep busy and some of your days seem too short to fit in all your interests.

Reading and philosophizing are two of your favorite pastimes. Any kind of book that helps you understand the world appeals to you. This is not to say that you are not interested in imagination—you most certainly are, and can find pleasure in fables, myths, and fairy tales, because they, too, contain important life lessons.

Sagittarians love to travel and enjoy trips because they provide a variety of learning experiences. You can be an ideal traveling companion for anyone who is as fond of far-off places as you are.

When you work, you prefer to wear old or utilitarian clothes, but when you dress up you have good taste. You like a home that has large rooms—you need ample space because you sometimes do, after all, enjoy entertaining.

You occasionally become weary after a series of ordinary days or a perceived lack of interesting stimuli. At work or at play, you like to have another person close by. This inspires you to excel. You like to tell others about your ideas, and the highest compliment anyone can give you is to listen appreciatively to what you have to say and tell you that you have caused them to look at things from a different perspective.

You are an excellent teacher of adults and children. Your philosophy of life is to help others make the world better by exposing people to the

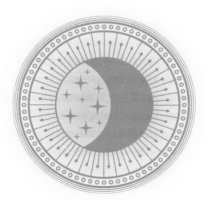

world's best practices. They remember the illuminating viewpoints you express or the inspiring messages that you share.

Because you can make up your mind quickly, you usually have your answers ready long before others can formulate their ideas. This makes you appear very intuitive. You also have a retentive memory, so you can supply facts and information rapidly.

What you say sounds interesting, rather than didactic, because you can add sparkle to any conversation. Frequently, you banter with friends and relatives as a reprieve from having to listen to family problems, gossip, or the news, a subject that drives you crazy because it merely dumps things in your way without giving in-depth context or coherent solutions. You would rather tell a joke than allow yourself and those you care about to be victimized by the gloom and doom of the media.

You have profound beliefs, but sometimes your casual attitude gives the impression that you lack respect for your own customs. Your respect and tolerance are real and genuine. You are just trying to gather best practices from around the world.

You have high ideals in love, yet you can be impersonal in your expression of affection. It is only on special occasions that you show your true commitment. It is impossible for you to compromise in a relationship where antagonism exists.

You value friendships highly. You want your friends to be as sincere with you as you are with them. You get along well with people in many walks of life, regardless of age or political affiliation.

·· LOVE AND RELATIONSHIPS ··

By keeping an open mind to factors that others might overlook or find too strange or foreign, you will seize opportunities to learn about people in a way that will make you very attractive.

Nature excursions are great for your mind, body, and spirit. For your well-being, you need to increase your awareness of the world around you. You might find love in the great outdoors, or by participating in or even watching sporting events.

If you do not have a relationship but want one, travel may bring one to you. Learning a language, going online, taking a class, or going to the library or other places to learn would also expose you to new ideas and people. You might even find yourself involved with someone who is from a different religion, race, or culture, or a faraway part of the world, or who is involved in broadcasting, publishing, travel, philosophy, or research.

Your love life could be negatively impacted by people outside your relationship having too much influence on it. This may be manifesting as one of you seeming to be under the control of a close friend or family member. This can make you or your partner feel less important than this other person.

Another risk is too much physical separation. One of you may be spending too much time away, either at work, with friends, or with family. Or your sense of privacy may feel violated when you realize your partner is talking about your private affairs with others and acting on their advice, not on yours. No matter what the problem, take the high road and avoid being a cliché.

As a Sagittarius, you will always be as honest and direct as you can be. Even if you have something negative to say, try to do so without hurting anyone's feelings. However, if there are any bad intentions involved, you should identify and avoid them.

Changes you make within yourself will be seen and felt as changes in your experience of the world, bringing into your life the kind of relationship where you each understand and respect each other's views.

Always be mindful to keep good boundaries between your relationship and your friends and family.

·· WORK AND CAREER ··

It is important to you to constantly improve your education and job skills, and especially your management skills. One thing you have to learn is how best to delegate. It's not that you do not trust others to do a good job. The problem is that you want to experience every task and the opportunity for growth that each affords. It is good to expand your mind about what is possible for you. Your curiosity about what is over the horizon should extend to your work and career.

Either you bring the world to you through the internet, newspapers, books, television, radio, and wireless technologies, or you take yourself to the world through travel. You might even find that you expanded your career opportunities by taking a trip.

You would do well to seek a job that is involved with the dissemination of knowledge, philosophy, and other information, as in the publishing, broadcasting, internet, and communications fields, as well as anything to do with the travel industry. Working outdoors, in sports or fitness and with horses or other animals, would also be an ideal job. Other professions that would be good include research, philosophy, education, film (especially documentaries), and writing books, as opposed to articles. Whatever you do, it would be a good idea to approach it as a lifelong learning experience rather than a job.

Going hand in hand with expanding your perceptions about the world is an appreciation for what the word *truth* really means. As you expand your understanding, you will better understand the word truth, and realize that for each person, truth reflects the unique position they are in. Accept this fact and you will succeed more quickly.

Break out of any boring routines, but avoid the appearance of disparaging those who prefer a predictable routine. If it is possible for you to obtain any kind of on-the-job training or schooling outside of work, by all means do so. If you are unable to do a job that interests you, increases your skills, or furthers your education, it may be time to look for another one, without leaving until you have the other job in hand.

If you are able, travel overnight for your work, transfer to a distant location, or maybe even work in a foreign country. It is important to find out how people around the world approach your job or their equivalent of your job. You may find valuable help in advancing your career by incorporating the best ideas the world has to offer.

You may be called upon to teach others the skills you possess. If you are asked, do so. Your interaction with your students will end up teaching you many things. It will also remind you of what you may have forgotten. The polarity of learning and teaching is very important to your career and should be pursued at every opportunity.

It is also as important that you seek the truth as it is that you speak your truth. Remember that your truth is not necessarily "the Truth." This concern for truth would make a career involving the justice system or journalism a very smart move. It would give you an outlet to be able to tell the truth to all, as well as to hear the truth spoken equally bluntly to you by others. Just remember that discretion is often the better part of valor, so keep your job and career on track by remembering that there is a time to speak and a time to keep quiet.

· · WEALTH AND SUCCESS · ·

Your honesty, directness, and ability to think big can pay off. Take time to learn about the lifestyles of successful people. Success and wealth can be real for you, and the more you study, the more you will learn the realistic trade-offs that come with the territory.

Your good fortune is most likely the result of your hard work. But, to other people, you may be seen as possessing pure luck. Your Sagittarian optimism might give the impression that you are doing better than you actually are, and you might have to learn what it is to have other people think you have it all.

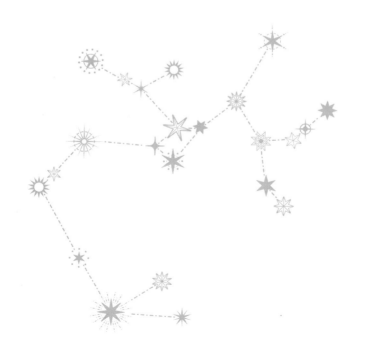

All manner of contests, awards, and prizes are favored for a Sagittarius, but especially the ones that expand your awareness or involve travel. Indulge your wanderlust whenever possible. The money you spend will come back to you multiplied.

Opportunities from far away may present themselves to you. In fact, people born in countries or in cultures very different from your own are most likely to benefit you. Their philosophy of life will expand your way of looking at things, and you will become aware of opportunities that you would have otherwise missed.

Even in your routine dealings with people, both at work and at home, there may be fantastic opportunities to learn or teach new ways of doing things. Be very generous and tolerant of others. In this way, you will gain their trust and confidence. They will protect you from any false rumors that may follow you as a result of your good fortune.

Your expanded awareness will enable you to deal with any petty jealousies. Not only should you have more sympathy for and from those you might have envied, but you should also extend your compassion to the less fortunate. Always remember your roots and how far you have come. Not doing so will inhibit the flow of wealth and success to you.

Wealth and success may come to you through sports, everything that is natural and pure, animals (especially horses), natural foods and remedies, healing, philosophy, travel, justice, social media, podcasting, broadcasting, and publishing.

If there are children in your life, work to ensure they will have a higher education waiting for them when they are ready. Scholarships and all manner of investments designed to pay for higher education are favored for Sagittarians. It may be your mission to broaden their horizons. Giving them the means to travel would be good, although traveling with them would be best.

SUN IN CAPRICORN

(DECEMBER 22–JANUARY 19)

QUALITY *Cardinal* → | **ELEMENT** *Earth* ⊕

Capricorn is known as the sign that wants to learn the best ways to achieve success and happiness. This is true, but what Capricorns truly need is respect, both from themselves and others.

Capricorns know in their hearts that they have much to learn before they can attain their full potential. Without feeling respected, Capricorns will, instead, be prone to depression, which some psychologists say is anger turned inward. When they respect themselves and are respected by those they value, there is little that a Capricorn cannot accomplish.

When you consider a change, you try to figure out beforehand whether you will be satisfied with the results. If you are in a situation where you doubt yourself more than you should, considering your options can actually turn into a form of obsession, causing you to ruminate until you become exhausted and exasperated. Capricorns generally apply this principle to all phases of their life. Only awareness of this tendency can help you overcome it.

You see no purpose in doing work or in buying things unless they are durable and effective. The things you wear are of good quality that will survive the test of time, rather than stylish, disposable, and cheap. You prefer to rely on your strong, serious, and dependable nature to make the right kind of impression on others.

The same is true of the furnishings in your home. You like well-made pieces. The books you read are informative and relate somehow to authority, especially to help you become one. You do not waste time on subjects that you do not find significant.

You find relaxation in thinking about ways to improve your results. You are interested in meeting people whose interests are similar to yours. You have a faculty for telling great stories with a wry and often sarcastic sense of humor.

Paradoxically, you appear more youthful with time. When you were young, your serious expression and apparent willingness to take on responsibilities beyond your years may have made you look older. Also, Capricorn's hard work pays off in the long run, and that attainment of financial or business success during maturity can free you from tension about the future.

When necessary, you can be very shrewd. You try to be prepared for every contingency, and can become quite frugal. This is not because you are cheap. Your chief aim is to save enough to get through difficult financial cycles and, if possible, build assets that can protect you from the next round of adversity. Being debt free and the owner of land or

houses that are free and clear of mortgages means more to you than having a big bank account.

Your knowledge in business and your ability to learn from your mistakes make it possible for you to earn enough to carry out most of your ambitions. Another reason for your achievements is your perceptive, discerning, and suspicious mind. You rarely have to worry about financial uncertainties because you neither gamble nor take useless risks.

Quite often responsibility is pushed upon Capricorns, starting in their early youth. You accept its demands and obligations with conscientious self-assurance. It does not occur to you to shirk it or unload your duties on the shoulders of others.

You do not expect something for nothing. You are willing to work hard for the comforts and security that you desire. Discouragement and struggles fortify your firm determination. The keystone of your belief system is to keep going until your goals have manifested.

You are at your best in regular and methodical work, or at tasks that call for a high degree of accuracy, concentration, and organization. You should be able to do well in all aspects of business where you have responsibilities at a level you respect, as well as in medicine, law, education, agriculture, mining, and real estate.

Capricorns exercise by taking long walks, swimming, hiking, or climbing. You like to have ample time to think or observe without being interrupted by demands for your attention.

You try not to be dependent on others. Your respect for established experts, authorities, and old-money wealth is proof that you admire those who have become successful through the tradition of hard work and persistence that you, too, ascribe to.

You do not flatter others, although you exercise a certain diplomacy toward anyone who holds a position of authority. You try to remain on good terms with them so as to help your advancement. The Capricorn nature is geared to routine work that shows achievement of purpose.

You place considerable emphasis on tradition and nice manners. You maintain a respectful attitude toward others and you expect the same. People who are openly jealous or uncouth annoy you.

· · LOVE AND RELATIONSHIPS · ·

Problems for you or your partner at work could translate to problems in your relationship. Rich or poor, if you, your partner, or both of you are not working or enjoying the same level of success or career satisfaction, your relationship might suffer. Also, if either or both of you are not doing what you know you should be doing with your life, this will be a source of irritation that may even lead to depression.

If your relationship has been going through hard times, do what you can to try to make things better. Perhaps your drive to become recognized, your hard work, and your sacrifice of personal time have created the problems. If so, take a few days off to just be together. This applies to both love and business relationships.

If you do not have a relationship but want one, one may come to you through your interactions with father figures or authority figures. You may meet someone this way, or you may actually become involved with an authority figure of some stature. This could be anyone who is respected by you or more typically by a group of people you respect. Another way this might manifest is if you meet someone while you are in a position of authority or working toward one. Or your next partner could just be famous or infamous.

You may find yourself attracted to a person who reminds you of the parent you most respected or were disciplined by, or you could end up with an older partner. If you are in a relationship, you may be shocked to notice how similar your partner is to your parent. Or it may be your partner who notices the resemblance. This is just pointing you to the next area of life that the two of you are going to be working on together.

Capricorns may enjoy an element of teacher and student in a relationship. You need the respect and recognition of those you

WELLNESS AND MINDFULNESS FOR CAPRICORN

CAPRICORNS know how to be disciplined in matters of authority and long-range planning. They take action based on practical needs and the desire to be respected by those they respect. Learning how to deal with and become an authority is one of their most important lessons.

Capricorns like to set goals for themselves and make action plans. But when life overwhelms them, it is time to get in touch with their spiritual and sensual needs. They should make sure to get enough rest at night, and enough light during the day, especially in winter.

consider important in your life. We have found that this is so important and yet so rarely stated that it bears repeating.

Be mindful that support and understanding from your partner regarding your work and career advancement can strengthen your relationship. If your partner is not supportive of your career, it will cause great stress on you and your relationship. Perhaps investigate working together with your romantic partner in some way, such as by starting a new business altogether. In any case, do not quit your job until you are certain beyond a doubt that any new business could support you both.

· · WORK AND CAREER · ·

To get ahead, try focusing on your career goals even more than on your everyday job. You can advance yourself. The reason you are being asked to work so hard is so you can enjoy all the rewards that come to you later. You will enjoy them even more if you postpone everything but the essentials for a while to concentrate on your advancement. Sometimes it may be necessary to delay social engagements and recreation in favor of things directly connected with your career.

At some time in the past you demonstrated your ability to work well both alone and with others. You also made it perfectly clear that you could come up with innovative solutions to problems. You have made your way of doing things look easy, both to others and maybe even to yourself. However, you must take any and all necessary steps to get serious about your career if you want to go to the next level.

In order to do that, you must get serious about where you find yourself right now. You have all the resources you need to succeed if you adopt a serious attitude toward your career. Even if you end up leaving what you are doing, your move will be accomplished with resources derived from where you are today.

If you find yourself between jobs, present yourself to prospective employers as someone who has everything needed to do the job. It is very important for you to become employed, so take the best of any jobs you see become available. Work hard now and you will be able to enjoy yourself later. Look at the big picture and avoid dwelling on little things that will slow you down.

Be mindful of situations where you may be given the opportunity to show how worthy of a promotion you are. This could be a test for admission to the club of those who are richer and more powerful than you. They were once in your position and now they want to help someone like you. Help them decide that it is you they should be supporting. It might be more beneficial to show them how similar you are to them than how different you are.

Reassure those in a position to help you that you approve of them and would like to learn what they know and do what they do. Save reforms for a time when you have successfully established yourself and are in a position to really make a difference. Take a deep breath and allow success to carry you along like a log in a swiftly flowing river. Do not try to push the river where you want it to go.

·· WEALTH AND SUCCESS ··

Capricorns can do very well in life. Promotions, sales, raises, bonuses, and business loans are goals to pursue in the Capricorn mountain goat's climb up the mountain of success. Long-term investments can pay off and your long-term goals can be reached, but only with patience.

Contests and awards where you can be recognized for your accomplishments are favored more highly than those of pure chance, such as company-sponsored contests or awards for attaining sales goals. Well-known and established contests are also favored, as are prizes given to those who display excellent timing.

Visualize what it feels like to be an authority figure, a goal more important than possessions to most Capricorns. Enjoy and be grateful for all the rewards derived from your long climb to the top.

If that moment has yet to come, take the time to get in touch with your inner guidance system so you know exactly where you are going and how you will get there. Then you will be most likely to manifest your plans, be recognized for your achievements, and even rise in status. In later years, you may find yourself looked to for wise counsel.

If you continue to clearly visualize and affirm your goals, you will begin the journey to realizing your destiny. Those you look up to will recognize the positive changes you are making and do all they can to help you. Your efforts will be acknowledged and supported.

The recognition you receive may not always bring you the wealth you seek immediately, but it is more than likely that it will in the long run. Any honors you receive will help you command a higher price for your services in the future. For now, you should be concerned with putting together a structure for your future wealth, so that when it comes to you, you will know how to make the best of it.

If there are children in your life, teach them the importance of respecting themselves and others for both their inner strength and their outer achievements. Teach them that there is a time for everything, even being serious about attaining wealth and success.

One of the unfortunate consequences of the instant social media/ app-based/I-deserve-it-now-because-I-am-a-wonderful-person attitude that strangely unites the lazy in all generations is that they see the story of successful people presented in an instant or even just a couple of hours. They have no idea how much dedication, work, rejection, and self-motivation are necessary to build a successful life. Try to teach children what you know about the value of planning and patience. They will listen to someone like you, a person who will have gained the respect of those in their immediate circle and even beyond.

SUN IN AQUARIUS

(JANUARY 20– FEBRUARY 18)

QUALITY *Fixed* ◊ | **ELEMENT** *Air* ≋

You are "a citizen of the world." This statement is true literally as well as figuratively because you are interested in humanity as a whole and in people no matter where they live and what they do. Any plan for a better world has your interest, if not your actual approval, which is hard to earn, despite your friendliness. Your philosophy of life is to be a good friend to all who need and can appreciate your inventive ideas.

Aquarians are here to learn how to make real the future they can so easily see in their mind's eye, but their life does not always provide them with as many opportunities as they would like to turn their innovative ideas into reality. Rising to this challenge helps define an Aquarian's life.

You try to discard outmoded ways of doing things as soon as new methods come along. Although you respect tradition, you believe in making progress as soon as possible—now, preferably. You do not want ancient customs and traditions to interfere with improving the living and working conditions for the people who are alive now.

Aquarians are the inventors and scientists of the zodiac. You like to experiment in every area of your life. When results do not turn out as expected, you keep experimenting until you are satisfied that you are doing something in a better way. This is how Aquarians get the reputation of always being ahead of their time.

The symbol for the sign of Aquarius is an old man lifting a big jar of water and pouring it out for everyone to drink from. Aquarians put their ideas out there for everyone to consider and implement, not just those close to them or a privileged few.

Aquarians try to show others how to help themselves, and how, by improving personal conditions, it is possible to reduce the difficulties in the lives of all people. You believe in the power of applied knowledge. Much of your time is used treating life as a laboratory and letting daily life inspire your innovation.

You study world trends. This awareness is activated by the fact that the world has just started the new two-thousand-year universal cycle known as the Aquarian Age. You are broadminded and ethical. You dislike any manifestation of selfishness, prejudice, or intolerance.

When it comes to their ideas and the implementation of them, Aquarians do not care what anyone says; they know what they know.

Yet you have a strong desire to be appreciated. Association with people of above-average intelligence, achievement, or ability is important to you because you have no use for ignorance.

You like to invite friends to visit you on special occasions, but at other times you want to work without interruption. The Aquarian train of thought can be easily derailed. When the unexpected throws your routine out of kilter, you try to make up for lost time without disclosing how much you have been inconvenienced.

You are practical and methodical in the management of household matters. You make constructive plans in advance. Your family's needs have top consideration, as do your home's requirements. You do not defer mending a leak in your roof until a rainy day comes along, nor do you wait to be asked for a favor before you grant it. Aquarians think about the future all the time. Usually you anticipate things that have to be done and waste no time.

You have an impersonal attitude toward yourself. This makes it possible for you to refrain from self-pity when you experience difficulties. Even when things go wrong for you, you do not impose on others. You try to work out your own problems. It is easier for you to plead for the benefit of others than to ask for help for yourself.

Aquarians are particularly good in a crisis and will not let themselves be rattled or show emotion until the crisis has passed. Strangely, long after the crisis has passed, they will get angry or show the emotions that have been kept in check.

Aquarians are not prone to showing their emotions, and this gives them the reputation of being cold. While it is true that they keep emotions in check so as to see clearly what must be done, they do have emotions, they are just not comfortable sharing them.

Aquarians are the rebels of the zodiac and must be careful not to "throw out the baby with the bathwater," or discard traditions that have a real and powerful purpose. They must learn to accept what is good about the past to help make a better future.

Aquarian rebels cannot condone anyone trying to limit their freedom in any way and they abhor even minor deceits. You allow everyone the right to their opinions, and you expect the same consideration of your ideas, because your aspirations are high and backed by the determination to make them into realities. You want your efforts to have a purpose and show progressive development.

You possess an inventive, out-of-the-box way of thinking and a limitless imagination. You can make spontaneous decisions based on constructive reasoning. This makes you popular among all types of people who like to consult you before setting their plans into motion.

You live easily in the present, while being guided by a keen vision of the future. You are able to keep to a fairly regular routine. You have the patience to concentrate on details, though when there are too many details and not enough chances to set your mind free, you will rebel and may abandon an important project or leave work unfinished.

Despite your friendliness, there are times when you are lonely. Boring conversation or monotony only aggravate the situation. Your concepts are too big to be restrained by a herd mentality. Whenever possible, you try to get away from restrictive attitudes or environments. You feel elated when your mind is unfettered.

· · LOVE AND RELATIONSHIPS · ·

Aquarians are the rebellious inventors of the zodiac and so they sometimes invent new relationship structures and can be very experimental sexually. Matchmaking events or dating websites would be favored.

If your committed partner, lover, or business partner is also your friend, then you can expect great things. If your partner is not a friend, then try to change that now or you may be in for an unsettled time.

All too often people are less kind, understanding, or forgiving to those they love than they are to their friends. If this is your situation, you must change things or you could end up changing partners.

If you do not have a relationship but want one, a friendship could blossom into a romance. Or you may find love through a friend's help. In existing relationships, it is very important that you treat each other with loving forgiveness and understanding. For an Aquarius, a relationship without friendship is in danger of failing.

Getting involved with groups of people who have come together for a common goal could help you find a relationship. This can be through your circle of friends, or through organizations, societies, clubs, unions, activism, social media, tour groups, group therapy, and all other ways that people get together for mutual support.

Though passion is important in a relationship, it would be great if the two of you also shared a passion for a particular goal. Planning for the future is another important part of relationships for Aquarians. A relationship where the focus is more on the past than on the future may not be successful for you. The exception to this would be if you confronted your partner and they were able to look at the situation dispassionately, realize the truth of what you are saying, and take real steps to change their behavior. Aquarians can do that, like a scientist having to admit that a new experiment has proven them wrong.

If you are having relationship problems, it may be that you or your partner is afraid that the next stage in your relationship will require sacrifice from one or both of you. So don't resist doing what you must to bring your relationship to the next level.

If you do not have a loving relationship in your life, you may fear that having one will require you to give up your independence and an exciting life. It may be that in the past you felt smothered and imprisoned by what you thought was love. You may have felt confused about yourself and your own needs and so you could have become attracted to someone whose needs were obvious. In this way, you may have given up on your own hopes and dreams and devoted yourself to helping your partner accomplish theirs.

Be mindful to become yourself as fully as possible. Invent a way to have a relationship that you can live with. It may not be conventional, but it will be a unique statement of your individuality.

· · WORK AND CAREER · ·

Work that allows you to accomplish new and exciting things will do well for you. Include the unexpected in your planning.

If you are set on a particular path to attain a career goal, you must expect things to take far longer than they would if you allowed room for the unexpected to work its magic. You must look within your heart to see whether your attachment to this method of attaining your goal is slowing you down.

Take note where readjustment is needed. You should always be open to new ideas regarding your career. Remember that each person is unique: each of us is a living example of a different truth about life. If you assume you know how things are going, you will not be open to the new opportunities that are all around you.

Allow yourself to remove your nose from the grindstone sometimes so you can look up and see how the world around you has changed. Things could be different now and what was true for you in the past is no longer so. Get as comfortable with change on a personal level as you are with societal change.

If you do not have a job or are thinking about changing careers, try working for groups that have organized for a common goal. There are many

WELLNESS AND MINDFULNESS FOR AQUARIUS

AQUARIANS have original and somewhat radical ideas about how to benefit humanity. Therefore, learning how to slow their active minds and preserve what is worth keeping while innovating new ways of doing things is the most important mindfulness lesson for Aquarius.

Aquarians are forward-thinking, open-minded intellectuals who love free-flowing ideas. Green tea with lemon and manuka honey helps promote sustained energy release and will fuel this sign's inventive thinking. They need lots of fresh air and pure water.

variations on this theme, but some would be trade unions and associations, credit unions, political groups, environmental groups, and other causes.

By being too set in your ways, you could become stuck in a rut. The minute you begin to think about new ways of doing things, you will see some of the possibilities for change. It will be like taking the first breath of spring air; when you feel that marvelous feeling, you will know that career improvement is on the way.

Take the time to correct your course of action. Like priming a pump, it is necessary for you to bring the first few small changes into your life. Do not get stuck in wanting things to turn out one particular way. It is important for you to be open to changing your plans.

One way to bring newness would be to volunteer for things you might have avoided in the past. Put yourself in a position where opportunity can find you. A job that involves more travel or exposure to unusual situations would really help get your career flowing.

·· WEALTH AND SUCCESS ··

As an Aquarius, you may be able to profit from an invention or original idea. With your Aquarian personality, you often need to reinvent yourself several times over the course of your life. Making new friends will usually aid this process. When you do, you will be able to look at yourself through fresh eyes. You will be able to put your best foot forward and get a chance to examine what it is you value about yourself. Think outside of the box and you will usually find new ways to increase your prosperity.

Wealth and success are likely to come your way through clubs and associations. Interact with those who share a common interest. Listen to any advice they want to give you about realizing your dreams and reaching your potential, even if it seems eccentric.

Any award or contest whose payout will be stretched out into the future would do well for you, as would those with a connection to astrology, numerology, or the science of numbers. Games and prizes with a scientific, space, futuristic, or historic theme would be more likely to pay off.

Note that your good fortune is most likely to come to you through your friends. They may bring you good fortune in the form of a gift or advice that you can profit from, or they may be the ones increasing their wealth and will share it with you.

If you are disturbed by the prospect of accepting gifts and other help from your friends, you must examine the standard you are holding

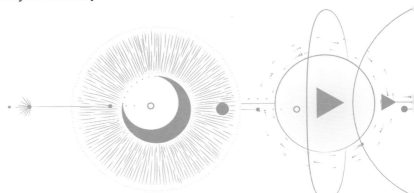

yourself to. When did you first think that being helped was weakness? Are you expecting yourself to be better than it is humanly possible to be? Are you the kind of person who likes to share good times with your friends? Then why not let them help you?

If you have ever sat around daydreaming with your closest friends, then those are the dreams most likely to come true. People who treasure your friendship have remembered your hopes and wishes and may have come across a unique way to make your dreams a reality.

Friends from the past may reenter your life at important turning points. Though you may not want to pick up just where you left off, it would be in your own best interests to see what they have been up to. It is good for you to be reminded of the things you used to wish for. You will be surprised to see how many of them you have gotten. Being aware of how far you have come will help you with your next moves.

If there are children in your life, show them there is a bit of the genius or eccentric in you. If you have been noticing a child getting too wrapped up in their personal life, it would be good to expose them to humanitarian goals. More importantly, share with them how humanitarian goals are reached by interacting with individual people, not by looking at humanity as something separate. It would be wonderful for you to teach and learn, on a new level, the importance of looking at each situation as if you have seen it for the first time.

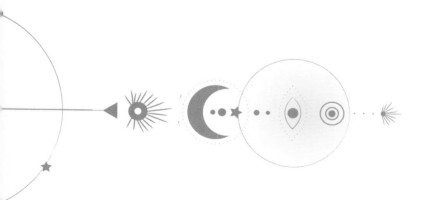

♓

SUN IN PISCES

(FEBRUARY 19–MARCH 20)

QUALITY *Mutable* ≈ | **ELEMENT** *Water* 💧

People born under Pisces have to learn how to get close enough to others to be of assistance to them without becoming overwhelmed by their needs. Pisceans may fear that the world will expect more of them than they can give, but the truth is that Pisces gives more than any other sign. The more honest and honorable a Pisces is, the more they hesitate to engage fully because they believe it might cause them to put their own needs second when they can ill afford to do so.

When your surroundings become chaotic, you like to withdraw to a secluded place where you can relax and think quietly. During these hours, you work out your creative ideas and blend them with the emotional effect you intuit will come to pass if you actualize your plans.

Your meditative moods have to be handled carefully, however, to avoid self-effacing behavior and unhealthy inhibitions. Too much isolation can cause a sense of loneliness or self-pity. Each can prove a serious impediment to your happiness.

It is to your advantage to do constructive work and live in a pleasant atmosphere. You pick up on the emotional vibrations of other people even through the walls of a home or apartment. Strife disturbs you and lack of useful service makes you restless. Your emotional stability depends on your ability to put the brakes on runaway emotionalism.

Because you are sensitive to the needs of others, you have the ability to succeed in work that includes service. The healing arts or social welfare are excellent professions for you because you have the temperament to be kind and sympathetic. You also could try teaching, acting, art, or precision work. You depend on your intuition regarding the mechanics, timing, and details of each task.

In business, you understand how to please your customers, and how to keep the atmosphere inviting. People enjoy the quality of the service you provide because you enjoy being of service. During your leisure hours, your preference is for hobbies that do not demand strenuous activity. You can become absorbed in almost any type of pastime.

One of your favorite diversions might be dancing. You are graceful because it is easy for your feet to follow rhythm and flow. The seashore or quiet places adjacent to lakes and rivers appeal to you. You like to spend much of your spare time at home or alone with a special someone outdoors. In fact, you can become so absorbed in your part-time activities that you are likely to neglect your regular job.

You do not like to become involved in an argument. However, you can insist on your rights and become surprisingly aggressive when you are disturbed in one of your frequent reveries or when someone you care about is hurt. You believe in the Golden Rule of "doing unto others as you would have them do unto you." For that reason, you feel upset when you have to struggle against lies or deception. Your biggest problem, however, is self-deception caused by allowing your daydreams to help you escape what needs to be done.

You can keep secrets, but you do not like to be in the dark about facts that you feel should be shared. It bothers you to come across a puzzle that you cannot crack. You enjoy solving a mystery.

You have an excellent memory and can recall events as if you were reaching back in time and experiencing them again. To an extent, the long-range recollections are bolstered by your strong intuition, sometimes seeming to be extrasensory perception.

Although you have a strong urge for daily seclusion, you do not like to live alone. For that reason, you want to be in constant touch with the members of your family and with trusted friends.

You are devoted to your loved ones. This can reach the point where you become dominated by someone more aggressive. You give in readily to the demands that are made on you, but you become disturbed when you are prevented from following a daily routine.

You can be indifferent to style, yet you achieve a remarkable appearance by wearing soft grays and pastel shades. The fabrics you select enhance the qualities of your nature. Faith in spiritual forces guides you throughout life. It is as if you feel this divine power in your consciousness, to guide you as well as to teach and comfort others.

· · LOVE AND RELATIONSHIPS · ·

Relationships where you share a passion for religious, spiritual, or even psychic phenomena would benefit you. If you are not in a relationship, then try attending events related to these themes.

Be very careful not to escape into a world of your own. The desire to experience other worlds should not keep you from fulfilling your practical obligations. Escape through the use of drugs, alcohol, sex, or any other addictions must be avoided at all costs. These shut out our reality and blur or destroy our identity. Be mindful that it is only through facing reality that we can grow in such a way that our expanded consciousness stays with us.

Because you have a giving heart, some type of sacrifice may be asked of you, your partner, or both of you for a larger purpose. One or both of you may be involved with a large institution and needs help with that situation.

WELLNESS AND MINDFULNESS FOR PISCES

PISCES knows how to flow with life's shifting changes. They are highly sensitive and empathetic to the emotional needs of others. Therefore, learning to keep their sense of self and set boundaries while helping others is one of the most important mindfulness lessons for Pisces.

An impressionable Pisces will relish the benefits of a reflexology foot massage, which addresses the energy points for all the organs in the body. They should always make sure they are well hydrated and keep their distance from negative or agitated people.

Events may make it hard for one or both of you to cope with the situation, and therefore you must support one another. If this mutual support is lacking, then you should try to do what you can to correct this problem. If there is no hope of that happening, then you may have to sacrifice either your relationship or your right to enjoy your life.

The element of sacrifice does not fit easily with the standard view of courtship and romance. However, the exception to this would be if you were dedicated to helping others or you needed help and met someone because of that. If you were both on the helping end, this would be more prone to lasting than if one of you was helping the other person. This would not be a relationship founded on mutual support, so it might need substantial reworking if the person receiving help no longer needed it.

The early dawn might be when you start or strengthen your relationships. Finding someone who enjoys meditating with you at sunrise would indicate that you have met a person with whom you are very compatible. Getting involved with religion, charities, the government, corporations, or other large institutions would be a great way to improve your love life and your love of life.

Be very mindful that, too often, denial is used as a way of avoiding an unpleasant reality. Many people would rather convince themselves that they are in a fine relationship, when it is actually doing them no good, than admit their problems. If they did disclose how hurt and angry they were, then they would have to admit that they were either too afraid to do something about it or too afraid to get out of the relationship. It is surprising how many people will resist facing up to their responsibilities.

Even one of the most spiritual forces in the universe, forgiveness, may be used as a disguise for denial and weakness. If there is alcohol, drugs, abuse, violence, or adultery standing between you and the truly loving relationship you dream of, you cannot deny or condone these dangerous and destructive forces forever. You must face what is happening and take immediate steps to correct the problem. If the damaged person will not do what is necessary, then you should get out of the situation. You can forgive at a distance, too.

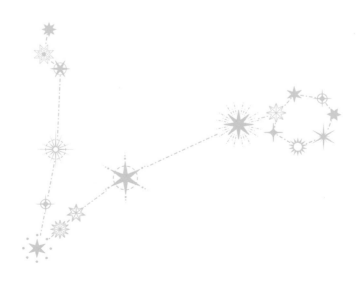

·· WORK AND CAREER ··

No matter what job you find yourself doing, you can reap great rewards by being sensitive to the needs of others. It may be that you are giving more than you are getting in return, but that is just the way things appear. Helping others who are deserving is one of the surest ways of bringing good fortune to everything you do.

It is crucial that you feel emotionally fulfilled by your work. Work that is too coarse or hurtful to others could make you feel upset or ill. If you are forced to be around people who are emotionally unstable, mean, or negative, you might feel yourself taking on these emotions. Shield yourself from these people's presence by visualizing that a suit of armor made from pure white light protects you.

Pisces often go with the flow and put their own needs second to those of the common good. Any freely given sacrifice could work to your benefit later. However, sacrifice with the expectation of benefit would substantially lessen any advantage that might come to you. Be like a worker ant, not a queen bee.

It would benefit you to be a small part of a major effort. Working with large institutions such as the government, hospitals, the armed forces, large corporations, organized religions, global movements, or charitable causes would be very good for you. It is necessary for you to get to know how people less fortunate than you feel about life. You are going to have to feel what they feel to do the best job you are capable of. While you may find some of the things you learn a bit shocking, the benefit to your career will be great.

If you are between jobs, applying for help at a large institution, especially one dedicated to helping others, would be suitable. Until your new job comes through, it would be highly beneficial for you to volunteer your services. A new and exciting career might come to you as a result of your volunteer work.

Without going overboard, you can assist those less fortunate than you. First, make sure the people and causes you are serving are truly deserving of your assistance; if you feel that they are, do what you can.

Whatever job you do, it is crucial to spend some time alone every day. Escape into your own private world to lessen your stress level. Try meditation.

·· WEALTH AND SUCCESS ··

Spirituality is derived from the fact that when we go looking for who we really are, we find that to a large degree we are not our bodies—we are our spirit. Our spirit is our true wealth and cannot be taken away from us. We can, however, sometimes forget our spirit and its power.

We can visualize wealth and success all we want, but we will have more luck if we put our heart and mind and body into the equation, too. If we think that there is something unspiritual about having money, then we will never allow our spirit to have the abundance that is our birthright. We must always remember that we have power over our reality through our thoughts and our willpower. Our willpower is stronger than our bad habits.

Success for you will often be determined by how much you are doing to help others, especially those less fortunate. Even if you do not have much to share, give what you can.

Success through interactions with corporations and large institutions is very likely. You could succeed in areas of life where you are just a small cog in a big machine, not focused on yourself but on helping to keep everything moving. The government, the military, museums, hospitals, prisons, religious institutions, and charitable organizations are strong themes to bring you benefits. All of these organizations require people to sacrifice their desires for a higher purpose, and that is precisely the attitude that would benefit you the most.

Your faith can move mountains. Be mindful to allow larger forces to work through you for your highest good. In fact, it would benefit you to ask what outside forces think you would benefit from receiving. You will be given help in proportion to the help you give others.

Very big contests where you are an anonymous entrant, or raffles and other kinds of games where you are a number or other sort of nameless contestant could work in your favor. All contests and lotteries run by the government, museums, charitable organizations, and large corporations, as well as contests held to benefit those less fortunate, would also be favored.

Note that giving selflessly requires that you take time every day to be by yourself to restore your energy and process. Ask yourself whether you are helping people who deserve your help.

If there are children in your life, show them the value of working for a cause greater than themselves; show them the practical value of a charitable attitude. Children under the age of seven would really benefit from such gentle teaching, for they are closest to this loving and openhearted spirituality. By interacting with them, you will see ways for you to return to the quiet strength of child-like faith.

Moon Signs

Y OUR MOON SIGN is determined by which zodiac sign the moon was in at the moment of your birth. The moon sign represents our emotional component, what is now called our *emotional intelligence.* The moon also represents how you feel about emotions—both yours and those of other people—how receptive you are to others, how inclined you are to reflect upon what you are experiencing, how you feel about nurturing yourself and others, and more. It all depends on the sign the moon is in and its angular relationship to the other planets. It's also important to understand your moon sign in relation to your sun sign.

When you were born, the odds are against both the sun and the moon being in the same sign. If your sun and moon signs are the same, you are doubly likely to look out on the world colored by that particular sign. For most of us, however, the sun and the moon in our chart can be found in different signs.

Virtually all the birth charts you can obtain for free online will spell out which of the twelve signs of the zodiac is your moon sign, just as most of them also list your sun and rising signs. If you have a chart that does not spell out the moon's position, then look for the symbol that looks like a crescent moon and check the glyph next to it against the list of sign and planet glyphs (see page 25).

Some signs of the zodiac can blend harmoniously and some present challenges. This is why it is so important to know your moon sign as well as your sun sign.

For example, if your sun is in the emotionally cool sign of Aquarius and your moon is in the empathetic, sensitive sign of Pisces, as in Monte's chart, this blend of sun and moon energies would incline a person to be compassionate and understanding of people's resistance to accept the radical and often disruptive changes that Aquarian sun signs are famous for supporting and advancing.

Another example is if your sun is in the forceful and goal-oriented sign of Aries and your moon is in the harmony and beauty seeking sign of Libra, the way they are in Amy's chart, this blend of sun and moon energies would incline a person to add the pursuit of harmony and beauty to each of the many goals every Aries has, ranging from today's to-do list and all the way up to their life's goals. As with Monte's unemotional Aquarian nature, the moon in Amy's chart both softens and adds a rich dimension to how and why she directs her strong Aries willpower.

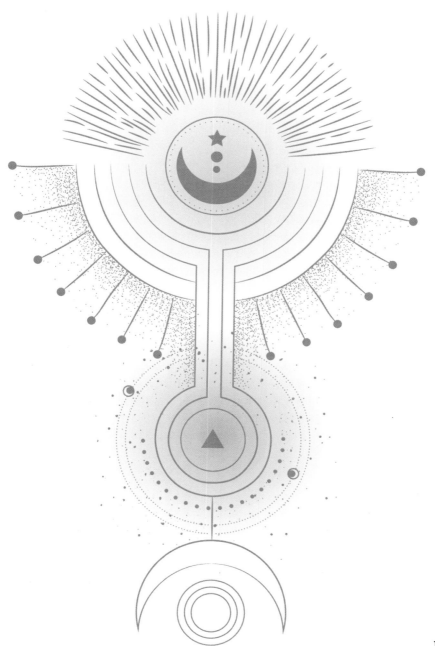

ELEMENTS

Fire 🔥 | *Air* ♒ | *Water* 💧 | *Earth* 🜨

To help you understand how your moon and sun signs combine, we would like to share with you an additional dimension of the twelve signs of the zodiac. We saw on pages 28–29 how the twelve signs are each classified under a quality as being either cardinal, fixed, or mutable. The signs of the zodiac are further classified into four groups of **elements**: fire signs, air signs, water signs, and earth signs.

The **fire signs** concern themselves with the realm of action, and each of them burns with a unique version of taking action to fulfill their desires and the almost unshakeable faith that they will succeed. The three fire signs are **Aries, Leo,** and **Sagittarius**.

The **air signs** concern themselves with the use of our rational mind to process our reality now and in the future, often based on a dispassionate view of our past, in the realm of ideas. The three air signs are **Gemini, Libra,** and **Aquarius**.

The **water signs** concern themselves with the powerful feelings that can produce tears of joy or sorrow, goosebumps of dread, or a connection beyond words, in the realm of emotions. The three water signs are **Cancer, Scorpio,** and **Pisces**.

The **earth signs** concern themselves with practical matters, the resources we can see, touch, or use to help us live successfully, in the realm of the material world. The three earth signs are **Taurus, Virgo,** and **Capricorn**.

INTERPRETING THE ELEMENTS WITH
YOUR SUN AND MOON SIGNS

To understand how your sun and moon signs blend together, you need only apply your understanding of how fire, air, water, and earth go together in daily life. If your sun and moon are in signs of the same element, then reread what we have written on the previous page about that element.

Add air to fire and your flame will increase greatly. If you add too much air to your fire you will either blow it out or cause it to burn much hotter than you had planned. That is not to say that any combination of air and fire signs will cause one's desires to be easily attained or focused. But sun and moon signs in any combination of air and fire will usually produce a person who "burns brightly" with passion and desire, and has within their being a surprising reserve of energy that can be used to keep moving forward despite obstacles. That energy must be used constructively and for the good of others, too.

Add water to fire and if the water is placed in the right vessel, you will have steam that can be extremely useful and powerful. If you add too much water your flame will go out. That is not to say that any combination of water and fire signs will see the attaining of one's desires extinguished by one's emotions. What it does indicate is that this individual has the ability to allow their emotional side to guide their ability to actualize their desires. They must always, however, be on guard to keep their emotions and those of their loved ones from overheating and overwhelming their ability to get what they want.

Add earth to fire and if the earth is placed in the right vessel, you can extract valuable minerals and other elements from various ores, from iron to steel and on to silver, gold, and platinum. If you add too much earth your flame will be smothered. That is not to say that any combination of earth and fire signs will see the attaining of one's desires extinguished by one's focus on practical matters or the monetary value of that focus. What it does indicate is that here we have an individual whose practical nature can be used to harness and guide the abundant energy they possess for the attaining of any goal or desire. They must always be careful to reflect on the perspective of others, to avoid making the mistake of forgetting to take others into account when planning to achieve their goals.

Add air to water and you get the beauty of the natural world, for they sustain all life that exists on Earth. Air and water can also combine into the destructive power of a hurricane or typhoon. That is not to say that any combination of air and water will see one's ideas drowned by emotions or one's emotions whipped up into a frenzy by ignorant ideas. What it does indicate is that here we have an individual whose ideas can be informed and guided by their emotions, something that often produces accurate hunches. They must always be on guard against the belief that any idea that produces a desired emotional response is absolute truth or something that can be used to get people to believe and feel as they do.

Add air to earth and the thing that comes to mind is a dust storm, but that is not necessarily true in a horoscope. An individual with sun and moon signs in any combination of these two elements is always informed and guided by their understanding of the real world and practical matters. They can use their logical mind to help them attain material success or make their way in the world by getting paid for supplying their ideas to others who need their expertise. They must always be on guard against seeing others as pieces on a chessboard to be used for their exclusive benefit. If they do

not keep this in mind, they may encounter strong opposition from other people with their own interests.

Add water to earth and you get mud, the primordial ooze from which life originated, and a substance that is often used by healers to draw out aches, pains, and even toxins. Mud can also impede progress and take the boots off of the strongest of adventurers. That is not to say that any combination of water and earth will produce a person whose emotions will dilute and undermine their practical nature. What it does indicate is a person whose emotions will sometimes be at odds with that practical nature. The best uses of this dynamic would be that this person's emotions would never allow their practical nature to act in a purely selfish manner or that this person could benefit materially from work to advance worldly matters that are in harmony with their emotions.

While your sun sign represents the core of your personality, what motivates and drives you, your moon sign is the key to understanding your sensitivities, emotional needs, and responses; how you want to be nurtured and how you nurture other people. These are the seen and unseen pieces of your psyche. Being mindful of how you shine and how you reflect is important.

The moon's sign in your birth chart points out how you process past experiences and the habitual strategies you have developed to deal with them. When you mindfully look below the surface and learn more about your patterns of behavior and deepest feelings, you become more reflective, less reflexive, and gain a higher perspective.

MOON IN ARIES

QUALITY *Cardinal* → | **ELEMENT** *Fire* 🔥

No one can tell you what to do! You are brave and a fighter, *especially when feelings are involved!* You are independent but you do not care whether others are. Others may try to get to you through your feelings because they know you'll act before you think. Don't let them manipulate you through your temper.

Power is an important issue for people with the moon in Aries. You are intelligent, quick-tempered, and courageous. You are self-reliant and your job may take you from place to place. You are much better at directing others than at being able to stick to details and routine. But make sure that you have mastered your own technique, so that you will be qualified to be "the boss." People with an Aries moon (or sun) are often considered bossy by other, less-driven signs.

The direct way in which you talk and the efficiency with which you come to your conclusions enable you to be a good leader. You could be a proficient teacher and ingenious inventor. But you are inclined to be too energetic to tie yourself down to one job. You want variety—and you manage to get it in work as well as in love. It takes a quick-moving and quick-witted person to keep up with your speed. When their emotions are allowed to override their logical mind, people with the moon in Aries can act before they think and end up having to use their creativity to fix situations that could have been avoided had they recognized that they had been triggered.

MOON IN TAURUS

QUALITY *Fixed* ◊ | **ELEMENT** *Earth* ⊕

You need comfort and security and prefer things to not change too much. You are loving and affectionate and *you need affection!* Only the best for you! Your tendency is to be calm and patient until you are pushed too far, and then watch out, world! Many people with moon in Taurus find it hard to get going, but once they are going they do not stop even if other people beg them to. People with moon in Taurus cope with situations that would send all the eleven other signs running for the exits. You want to show people how strong you are emotionally, but sometimes this results in your staying when you should be going. It is hard for you to change your feelings.

Having a plan and a system is crucial for you. You are determined, ambitious, and independent. You like to stay in one place, and this desire prompts you to invest in real estate. You like to own things, especially houses and tracts of land. You like music and often have a melodious voice. You become rather fixed in your habits and cannot tolerate deviation from your system. You should follow your plan so you can become independent.

You know what you want and why you want it. You have the courage to demand your rights because you seldom impose on others. When you accept a favor, you reciprocate in full. Your friends know how generous and kindhearted you are, but to others you can seem lazy and self-centered. It is difficult for you to rouse yourself into action unless you feel an emotional connection to what needs to be done.

MOON IN GEMINI

QUALITY *Mutable* ≈ | **ELEMENT** *Air* ≜

You are constantly alert and ready to experience life like no other moon sign. You want and need to communicate your feelings; not doing so is not good for any aspect of your being. You want to learn all, especially what's new and different. You are cool in a crisis, but your emotions change so rapidly you can become restless and bored during times of relative calm. Be careful not to talk about yourself too much.

Progress is the operative word for people born when the moon was in the sign of Gemini. To make it easier for you to achieve the consensus necessary for progress, your moon sign helps you have a flexible mind-set. You are candid, sincere, and, of course, progressive, though you have an ever-changing definition of that word. You are always busy, even when at rest. You can hatch more ideas in a given time than a dozen others put together, unless there is another moon in Gemini person among them. Your occupation will depend on your environment because you can do almost anything that interests you.

Your daily program is so arduous and so varied that it keeps others guessing how you manage to get any rest. But you can recuperate very quickly, and even when you appear to be going at full speed, you are more restful than is apparent to the casual observer. Moon in Gemini people have a unique ability to keep their emotions from running wild and causing them problems.

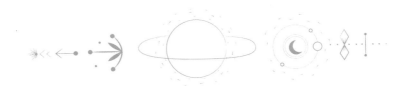

MOON IN CANCER

QUALITY *Cardinal* → | ELEMENT *Water* 💧

The sign Cancer is "ruled" by the moon. Because they go together perfectly, you are very emotionally intelligent. Mother(ing) is *very* important to you. You have great intuition and may use it in your work, whether that is as a counselor, an investor, or even an intuitive.

Feelings are more important to you than thinking, so remember to make the effort to use both in your decision making. If you are confronted too strongly or criticized, you have a tendency to retreat into your shell like the crab that is the symbol of your moon sign. If someone you care about is threatened, however, you will not hesitate to do everything you can to protect them from harm.

You have a very emotional nature if you were born when the moon was in Cancer. Where you grew up is important to you, and if you overcome your tendency to stick close to home, you may find your new place resembles your old one in some important way.

You take your obligations seriously and are close to your mother. She might depend on you, or you on her. In your own quiet way, you have great tenacity of purpose. You can express yourself through music and literature. You also like the sea.

Your very tenderness and emotional delicacy make you vulnerable to the barbs of treachery, so you must never expose yourself to anyone whose character cannot stand the acid test of loyalty. When you love, you do so genuinely. Therefore, it is only right that you should attract the same romantic devotion.

MOON IN LEO

QUALITY *Fixed* ◊ | **ELEMENT** *Fire* ◊

Just as with people with their moon in Aries, people with their moon in Leo cannot be told what to do, but unlike Aries people, who enjoy being on their own, you need an audience. Therefore, you need to be careful how you act while you inform others that you are going to do it your way.

You need to feel proud of yourself and will stand up for everyone and everything you are proud of. If circumstances prevent you from being your authentic self, you can make yourself sick and thereby give yourself the opportunity to subtly show your displeasure.

When you like someone, you tell them, and you want the same. You like to play and may sometimes tease someone, but if they do not see it that way, they will think you are serious! Be aware of how you consider yourself important; you may exaggerate or otherwise try to attract attention if your feelings aren't respected.

Even if they are of humble origins, people born with the moon in Leo have at least one of the attitudes or the mannerisms found in the nobility of olden days. You really are noble and strong-willed if you were born when the moon was enthroned in Leo. There is nothing petty or underhanded in your nature. You are candid, proud, able, and popular. You can be a good orator, a first-class executive, and a practical manager. You command the respect of your associates and they trust your judgment implicitly. You can think for yourself and for others.

Your royal lineage sets you on a pedestal for those who love you. You are used to having your own way, so much so that you sometimes are not as thoughtful as you might be. But few can be more generous and gracious than you. So, if you are self-reliant without being "bossy," you have molded your glowing moon traits into a radiant personality.

MOON IN VIRGO

QUALITY *Mutable* ≈ | ELEMENT *Earth* 🜨

You are an odd blend of happy and serious and can tip from one to the other for the strangest reasons. You have more skills than most people because you are careful and like to be useful. Like your unique blend of happy and serious, your usual neat and orderly nature can be put aside if you become upset; in fact, that is a good way for you and others to know that something is bothering you.

Be aware that you tend to analyze and worry about your emotions. It can make you wrongly believe that others don't like you, but they do. It's you who doesn't like yourself, just like most self-aware people, but with your tendency toward perfectionism you judge yourself more harshly than others, to the point where you actually punish yourself by denying yourself what you want or need. This tendency will lighten up if you lighten up and stop taking yourself so seriously.

Moon in Virgo people strive for competence. You are polite, reserved, and practical because you do not want anyone to interfere with you. You can adapt yourself to circumstances more than other moon signs, and your keen ability to analyze a problem logically and obtain the answer intuitively can be amazing, even to you.

You can be an excellent teacher and a patient guide; criticism is natural to you, so see if you can use this trait professionally. Your career should depend on your mental preparedness. You work well with others.

You are seldom hoodwinked because your keen mental perception enables you to detect a lie a mile away. Also, you are never fooled about the value of merchandise because you know prices as well as quality. You have an almost clinical memory that is unusually retentive and reliable. When you know something, it is so—and you can prove it through records and facts.

MOON IN LIBRA

Y ou truly feel that everything and everyone is beautiful in its own way. You are kind, affectionate, and a good friend. People like you. Peace-loving, you are so nice you may be fooled by liars and crazies. Don't give in to keep peace if you should fight for justice. Avoid laziness in both yourself and others who want you to believe that lack of ambition or avoiding work as much as possible is somehow noble or spiritual.

Dependability is something that you strive for and you require it in your partners. You are a clear thinker, warmhearted, faithful, loyal, and courteous. You dress well, have good manners, and do not consciously like to offend anyone, although you are aggressive when you decide to confront someone or something you consider to be unfair.

You are sincere when you make a commitment, especially when it comes to your marital vows. Your life mate is more important to you than anyone else in the world. Because Libra is the natural horoscope house that rules marriage, you can see what an important influence your life mate has on you and vice versa. Once trust is lost in that area, your fidelity can no longer be guaranteed. If you can resist the impulse to focus on weighing one feeling against the other so as to justify past or present actions, you can get a lot done.

MOON IN SCORPIO

QUALITY *Fixed* ◊ | ELEMENT *Water* ♦

Your feelings are intense, deep beyond words, and complicated. You need your life to be intense so that you feel justified and comfortable with your feelings. You are a born investigator, and no one can get anything by you, unless you let them. Moon in Scorpio people either love metaphysical (beyond the physical) studies like astrology for the powers they confer on those who know their secrets, or they hate the metaphysical because other people might be able to have some kind of advantage over them.

Others are confused by your moods because you are, too! Don't take your emotions too seriously. Take your passion seriously.

No one can discover or keep a secret the way you can, if you really want to. Avoid jealousy and exposing other people's secrets as much as you can. We would also caution you against trying to obtain some kind of revenge against someone you believe wronged you. Your emotions can lead you to sting yourself, like a scorpion does in the heat of battle.

When you have the moon in Scorpio in your chart, you are reserved, energetic, and persistent. You can be enterprising, choosing to follow ideas that are a puzzlement to those close to you, and you like to plan things that start small but have the potential to transform into larger enterprises. You like to associate with those who appreciate you and your abilities and will avoid those who do not, waiting for your chance to show them who you really are. You like to be at the head of all undertakings, and your foremost aim is to win success. More than any moon sign, you do not like to be an also-ran.

But you really are not so stubborn and self-centered as you seem to be. Actually, your courage and stamina to meet your problems as they come set you apart from those who lack willpower. It is they who criticize you most because in their hearts they envy you.

MOON IN SAGITTARIUS

QUALITY *Mutable* ≈ | ELEMENT *Fire* ◊

Y ou are an optimistic idealist, a deep thinker about the environment and natural laws, and a philosopher with your own ideas about the nature of a human being's personal reality. You want to travel and share favorite places with all. It is important for people born with the moon in Sagittarius to avoid losing their faith, which will make you feel empty and unable to find enjoyment when the world or individual people let you down. Take them as they are, the same way that you wish to be taken, and move on.

Someone with the moon in Sagittarius must always feel free to express their emotions as honestly as they can. If circumstances prevent this, they can find themselves feeling anxious, which can lead to colds or circumstances that prevent them from getting out in the world as much as they would like to.

You are broad-minded, sincere, and voluble if you have your moon in Sagittarius. You are quick, optimistic, and agreeable. This position frequently denotes prophetic qualities. You like animals, sports, and the social side of life. You are not a recluse and actually need to be able to get outside every day to feel complete.

You work well alone or with others and frequently have outstanding talents, especially the ability to have faith in your project, your team, or your organization—a true inspiration.

You are well informed and are better at mental than manual occupations. You take things as they come. When you miss a deadline or guess wrongly, you do not waste time in vain regret. You shrug your shoulders actually or figuratively and begin once more to plan, work, and hope. You are a natural hunter—always off on a new scent and a new quest. You are tolerant and kind, for Sagittarius is the astrological sponsor of philanthropy and the many ways of living found around the world.

MOON IN CAPRICORN

QUALITY *Cardinal* → | **ELEMENT** *Earth* ⊕

People born when the moon was in the sign of Capricorn are serious, cautious, and don't like fools or people who fool around when they should not be doing so. You are ambitious and practical. You need to feel respected and will work for it. You seem older than you are and may have been given too much adult work when you were young. The moon is associated with feelings in astrology, while Capricorn is more associated with tamping down one's feelings so that they do not interfere with one's goals, especially career goals. This is why moon in Capricorn people are more uncomfortable with their feelings than any other sign. You have high standards and when you do not live up to them, you are quite hard on yourself.

People with a Capricorn moon are prudent and economical, and they want to fit in with those who are respected, successful, or an authority in some way. You are a good administrator and although you like to be exclusive, you can mingle with others when it suits your purpose. Politics and business are areas of life where many moon in Capricorn people are found because that placement enables them to do what they have to do and not what they would like to do.

You take pride in being reliable. When you give your promise, you make every effort to keep it, even if it is not always convenient to do so. People know they can depend on you and that you will not let them down. This trait brings you friendly devotion or economic reward. This reputation is worth a good deal to you and you will do anything to preserve it.

MOON IN AQUARIUS

QUALITY *Fixed* ◊ | ELEMENT *Air* ≊

Aquarius is the least emotional of all the twelve signs of the zodiac, so it is not surprising that those born when the moon was in this sign are not comfortable with their emotions, but must hold them at arm's length and examine them the way a scientist examines an experiment. You need to feel in control and separate from your emotions if you want to be comfortable with them.

You must feel free to experiment and feel as you wish with whomever you wish. You control your feelings, but reveal them at odd times. Emotional displays and even affection can sometimes annoy you, though you are not sure why this is so. People with the moon in Aquarius are great in a crisis but often get surprisingly crabby after the crisis has passed.

You have a distinctively rebellious or otherwise unusual personality and a sociable though quiet nature. You can be emotional in a robotic way, though only those who care about you can tell when this is going on; you keep yourself under control as a rule. You often ally yourself with radical thinkers and enjoy being a reformer. You want your ideas and ideals to merge. You are a hard worker, but sometimes lack persistence if too many of the same boring details have to be attended to. You have a good deal of initiative and executive ability, however, so you can delegate.

You never stay down no matter what the setback to your hopes and aspirations. You have the instinct for rapid recovery. You rise above hindrances, limitations, and disappointments. Knowing that existence is too brief to curtail even a fraction of its joys and pleasures, you root for tolerance and freedom.

MOON IN PISCES

QUALITY *Mutable* ≈ | **ELEMENT** *Water* ⬩

You are kind, sensitive, and compassionate. If you can isolate yourself so you are not influenced by the energies of other people and can put your feelings in perspective, you will receive and use intuitive and seemingly psychic information. You are kind but need to be taught at an early age to only help the deserving. It is imperative that you avoid negative people because they will drag you down to their level. Use your imagination creatively, not for escape into a Utopian fantasy world that can never exist in reality.

Yours is a harmonious and composed personality. You like to have peace wherever you are. Strife and discord affect your health. You can express yourself easily and enjoy all the things that are beautiful and colorful. Your best work is done in quiet places. Medicine, art, religion, and service work call many who have the moon in Pisces.

You are so sensitive to the suffering of other people that when anyone of whom you are fond is in distress, you feel it with almost bodily impact. You cannot bear anything that is harsh, trite, or commonplace.

For someone born when the moon was in Pisces, life in all its phases must be harmonious and melodious because at heart you are a musician who plays your life as an instrument and an artist who paints reality with your existence.

Rising Signs

Your **RISING SIGN** is one of the most important things you will ever know about yourself. This sign, also known as your "ascendant" and abbreviated as ASC on most computer-generated birth charts, is the sign of the zodiac that was coming up/rising/ascending on the eastern horizon at the moment you took your first breath. The astrological meanings associated with your rising sign give a unique twist to your sun and moon signs. Your rising sign is about how others see you.

As you now know, your sun sign is how you look out onto the world, and your moon sign gives insight into how you respond on an emotional level to the world. Your rising sign, however, is how the world sees you.

That is crucial information if you are at all interested in interacting with others and making your way in the world.

If you have ever wondered why others seem to misunderstand you, this may be why. If your sun sign and your rising sign are very different and—here's where mindful astrology comes in—if you are not aware of how you are perceived by other people, you should not be surprised that people do not "get" you.

Most people have a rising sign that is different from their sun sign, the exception being those who are born around sunrise, in which case your sun sign is the same sign of the zodiac as your rising sign. In such cases, what people see is most often what they get.

Because misunderstandings between people lead to a lot of the human-caused problems in this world, a strong case could be made that our rising sign is actually more important than our sun sign. This is even more true in early life, because babies cannot speak and so how they are perceived by their caregiver(s) determines how they will be treated later in life. It is therefore *so important* for parents and caregivers to know the rising sign of their children.

We believe that every baby born should have their rising sign determined while they are still in the hospital and their parents be given a copy of this book, which has dedicated information for parents of young children. This one addition to the process of welcoming a new child to our world would change it profoundly for the better.

For example, Capricorn-rising children can be saddled with too much responsibility at too young an age. These children are more likely to assume positions of power, but many wield it to the disadvantage of all concerned because of their childhood experiences.

Knowing all the rising signs will also improve how parents and caregivers interact with their nonverbal charges and, therefore, improve the world we live in. All twelve rising signs are explained in detail in the following pages.

We know it takes time to get used to seeing the influence your rising sign has on your interface with the world. It's like seeing

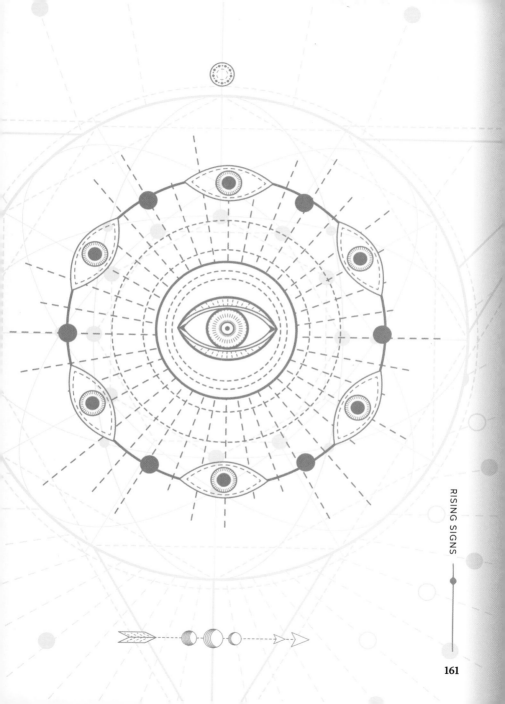

yourself in photographs after you have seen yourself in the mirror your whole life. You know it is you, but it is somehow different. We felt that way, too, when we first studied astrology many decades ago. Hear us out, read about your rising sign, and see whether what we are saying makes sense.

Your sun sign, the one you would read in a newspaper's horoscope column, is based on the day you were born, but your rising sign is based on the time and place you were born. The time and place of your birth is needed to determine exactly which of the 360 degrees of the zodiac is rising on the horizon at the moment of your birth, as viewed from where you were born.

If you were born at sunrise, then your sun sign was on the horizon when you were born and you are a "double" sign. The daily newspaper horoscope will be more accurate for you than for most other people. We should mention here that this "double" phenomena will also be true if your moon sign was on the horizon at the moment you first drew breath. If your sun, moon, and rising signs are all the same zodiac sign, then you are a "triple" of that sign, and what the world sees is almost definitely what they are going to get when it comes to you and how you relate to the outside world.

Most people are not born at sunrise; the odds against it are, naturally, eleven to one (there are twelve signs and only one can be your rising sign). The same is true about your moon sign. Most of us are a complex blend of different sun, moon, and rising signs.

Knowing that Monte is an Aquarius sun sign with a Pisces moon and the sign of Leo rising, and that Amy is an Aries sun with a Libra moon and Scorpio rising has enriched our lives immeasurably. Aquarians are usually described as eccentric, forward-thinking, emotionally cool, and aloof . . . wait! Emotionally cool and aloof? No one who knows Monte would ever say that about him, even when he was actually sending out the vibe of being cool and aloof inside his head. Why? Because he's a Leo rising, Mr. Fun and Excitement—think "show biz." Leo stage fright is being afraid when you are *not* on stage!

Leos, like their symbol, the lion, are prideful and look out onto their world as king or queen of the "jungle" in which they live, but their rising sign determines how the world perceives their strong ego and ability to lead. Leo risings enjoy showing the world how it's done. Leo risings are demonstrative to a fault, hence the reason no one who knows Monte would ever describe him as cool and aloof.

So, what good does it do Monte to know that he is an Aquarius sun with the sign of Leo rising? Well, for one thing, he never has to worry that someone finds him cool and aloof. Leo is the opposite sign to Aquarius, and so his Aquarian desire to make the world a better place is aided by his Leo rising, because Leo is the leader and you need people to be on your side if you want to have any influence on the world. Those with some of the other rising signs have a hard time interacting with others, even others whom they care deeply about, because their rising sign and their sun sign are not conducive to accomplishing their interpersonal goals.

Knowing your rising sign allows you to take refuge in it. When Monte is too in his head and distracted, like any good Aquarian, he doesn't have to worry that his mind being a thousand miles away will be seen for what it is. He is, in that case, free to be himself, and that freedom is probably the most important benefit to be derived from knowing how to rock your rising sign.

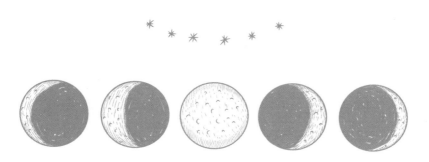

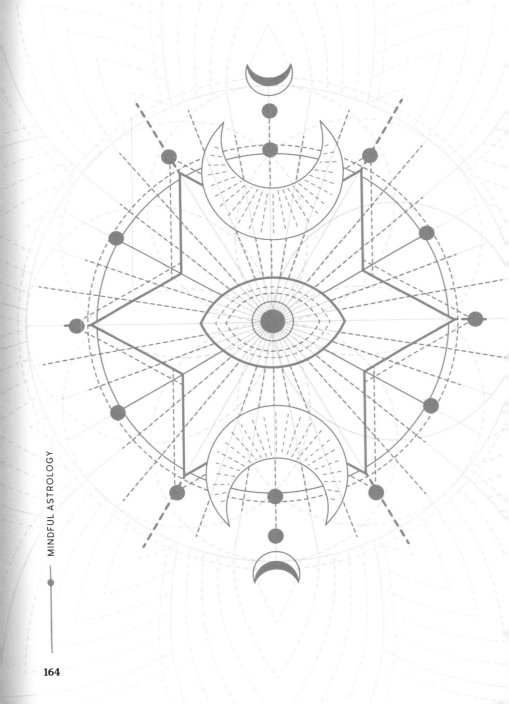

BASIC TRAITS OF
THE TWELVE RISING SIGNS

Explaining the concept of the rising sign is one of the most important aspects of *Mindful Astrology*. Until you know and understand the interplay between your sun, moon, and rising signs, you do not have a clear, effective, and useful understanding of how other people perceive you and relate to you (or not!), and you are unable to truly optimize your interplay with others. No matter what we do or don't do, whether we know it or not, our interface with the world is presented through our rising sign. This is why knowing your rising sign is so important; it's how other people see you, whether or not you want them to see you that way!

If the concept of the rising sign still seems a bit odd or hard to grasp, we suggest thinking of yourself as an old-school movie projector. When people went to a movie theater, there was a projector operated by a projectionist in a little room at the back of the auditorium. The movie projector was able to project the movie onto the screen for the audience to view using a very bright light bulb and a curved mirror that concentrated the light. That concentrated light was then shot through the transparent film and onto the projector's lens, where it shone out across the auditorium and onto a specially made reflective movie screen, where it appeared as moving images.

Remembering how a movie projector works, think of your sun sign as the light that shines out the movie of your life, your moon sign as the curved mirror that helps you concentrate and reflect your essence (the inner workings that no one necessarily sees), and your rising sign as the sum total of the film and lens that produces what your "audience" sees. You project your emotional intelligence (described by your moon sign) onto the world that's colored by your light (your sun sign), but the world only sees the image on the surface of the lens and the movie screen (your rising sign).

The nature of the rising sign and its planetary ruler determine your personality, mentality, physical appearance, and, to an extent, factors in your destiny. This explains the importance of correctly ascertaining the rising sign as best one can. Births are overwhelming and even times recorded on one's birth certificate can be off by minutes, sometimes more, so do not despair if you don't know your exact birth time. In our decades of experience, we have found that doing the best we can with the information we have is quite good enough for making accurate assessments and useful predictions.

The power in knowing your rising sign comes from understanding how what you're trying to say or do is being perceived. You can use that "image" as a shield, a battering ram, or otherwise modulate it according to what you want to accomplish. Being mindful of your rising sign and of astrology's teachings can help you live life to the fullest.

ARIES RISING

QUALITY *Cardinal* → | **ELEMENT** *Fire* ◊

It's easy for others to think you are either extremely self-confident or arguing with them. If you feel weak, no one knows. Dial it down when you want to be nice.

PHYSICAL APPEARANCE: Medium to tall; angular body; broad face, narrow at the chin. Sharp eyes with thick eyebrows. Complexion and hair sandy to dark.

FAVORABLE PERSONALITY TRAITS: Energy, enthusiasm, skill at promoting ideas. An inherent force and willingness that can help reach the top. Ambitious, proud, high-spirited, independent, and chivalrous.

ADVERSE PERSONALITY TRAITS: Domineering, conceited, impractical. Not good at sustained effort. Loses interest quickly, branching off into something else; often "fights windmills."

If you are an Aries rising, the good news is that people will always see you as honest, independent, and a go-getter who knows the best way to start a project, though once things get going you may appear anxious to move on to other projects.

People are inclined to interpret your words and your actions as forceful, passionate, and focused mostly on your need to be the boss in the situation at hand, even when this is not the case and you are not trying to give this impression. Those you encounter who have a negative view of people who present themselves and their ideas strongly may be put off by your manner.

Also, those who have a problem with seeing themselves as confident and powerful may go into full-on projection mode and react to you the way they dialogue with their inner self, getting overwrought and even outright angry with you for no apparent reason.

If you see or even sense this kind of reaction in someone you care about—and the reason you care can run the gamut from someone you love to someone who is important to your plans—you must dial down your natural tendency to bravely and energetically say what is on your mind. It is not cowardice to modulate your tone and choose your words with care. Discretion is the better part of valor.

It is fine to appear brave, strong, and aggressive when the situation warrants it. Keep in mind that not everyone feels comfortable with someone who seems so sure of themselves that they appear to have little or no regard for the beliefs of others. It is almost certainly not your intention to make anyone feel uncomfortable or afraid to be themselves with you, but be mindful of how your particular rising sign is well known to manifest.

More than almost any other rising sign, Aries rising needs to use their innate ability to be old-school pioneers to move into the uncharted world of individual interpersonal interactions with the same care an explorer would use in an unknown land. Even when you and those you interact with speak the same language and are based in similar locations, you must learn the nuances of language and the customs of those you encounter for a successful and enjoyable journey.

TAURUS RISING

QUALITY *Fixed* ◊ | ELEMENT *Earth* 🌐

It's easy for others to see you as slow and deliberate but dependable, desirous of life's luxuries. Use your "resting rich face" when not sure.

....

PHYSICAL APPEARANCE: Short to medium height; square frame with rounded contours; sometimes stoop-shouldered. Strong or beautiful neck; full lips; prominent eyes.

FAVORABLE PERSONALITY TRAITS: Faithful, practical, responsible, steadfast. Fond of home, adores children, usually agreeable and genial. Likes family life, good community standing, meticulous about paying bills.

ADVERSE PERSONALITY TRAITS: Stubborn, obstinate, likely to keep on to the bitter end, even if wrong. Undemonstrative and takes affection lavished upon them for granted. Sometimes coarse or neglectful of courtesy. Bad temper when aroused; "sees red" like a bull.

....

If you are a Taurus rising, the good news is that you will usually be seen as patient and kind. Your appreciation and knowledge about the good things in life will be admired.

When you are trying to work your will on the world, people will be inclined to interpret your words and your actions as being based on your desire to avoid change, discomfort, and personal loss. That loss can be of prestige, finances, or anything you consider to be valuable. As is the nature of the rising sign, you are likely to be perceived in this way even when you are not trying to give this impression.

Remember, however, that some people like to think way outside of the sturdy, self-protective box that Taurus-rising people strive to create and maintain. Those you encounter who have a negative view of people who are resistant to radical change, or who make rapid alterations to an existing plan, may be put off by your Taurus-rising ways of interacting with the world. Even if you are championing a potentially disruptive or revolutionary concept, it will take skill on your part to present it in a way that does not seem motivated by selfishness.

Those who have a problem with seeing themselves as dependable, persevering, and able to cope with difficult circumstances may react to you the way they dialogue with their inner self, stubbornly refusing to cooperate and even acting like a bull who sees a red cape.

If you see or even sense this kind of reaction in someone you care about, you must dial down your natural tendency to start seething as you dig in your heels at the first sign of someone trying to get you to do something that you do not want to do, especially to give up. As a Taurus rising, you will not be seen to be weak or easily discouraged even if you judge yourself to be so.

More than almost any other rising sign, Taurus rising needs to use their innate ability to keep moving forward, despite all obstacles, to inspire others or, if the opposite outcome is desired, to show that you are going to persevere and further resistance is futile.

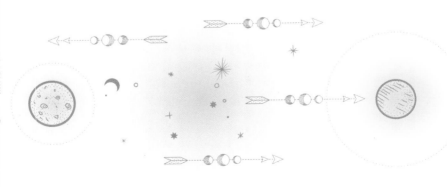

GEMINI RISING

QUALITY *Mutable* ≈ | ELEMENT *Air* ≜

It's easy for others to see you as smart, versatile, and changeable. Those with strong opinions see you as uncertain. Speak clearly and more slowly than you think you should.

....

PHYSICAL APPEARANCE: Height averages medium to tall. Usually slender and upright. Active gait; pleasant but penetrating eyes and pointed features. Long arms and fingers.

FAVORABLE PERSONALITY TRAITS: Brilliant, versatile, flexible, charming, stimulating, scintillating, and fascinating. Good at repartee; entertaining and amusing. A flair for writing fiction and telling stories.

ADVERSE PERSONALITY TRAITS: Irritable and quarrelsome. Expresses a point of view, only to change it the next minute. Frequently untruthful. Often suffers from nervousness.

....

If you are a Gemini rising, the good news is that you will usually be seen as smart, shrewd, and a fast learner. Your appreciation for and knowledge about the latest developments in virtually all aspects of modern life will be appreciated.

When you are trying to work your will on the world, people will be inclined to interpret your words and your actions as if you are inconsistent in your beliefs. You can be perceived on a spectrum, from appearing merely unconvinced all the way up to having a split personality disorder, as if there were two or more different people inside you and others cannot be sure which one they are going to get. As is the nature of the rising sign, you are likely to be perceived somewhere on this spectrum even when this is not the case.

Remember, however, that some people are firmly anchored to beliefs that they do not question, and many people simply need to arrive at a definitive conclusion before they can feel secure. Those you encounter who have a negative view of people who are prone to thinking out loud or otherwise giving the impression that they seek to see all sides of an issue may be put off by your Gemini-rising way of interacting with the world. Even if you are seeking to learn as much as you can prior to making a decision, problems can arise with other people because Gemini-rising people rarely appear to have arrived at a definitive view, a final decision, or even a reason to cease deliberating.

Also, those who have a problem with seeing themselves as open-minded, undecided, or able to see all sides of an argument may react to you the way they dialogue with their inner self, getting nervous and tongue-tied, sputtering words of resistance for no apparent reason.

If you see or even sense this kind of reaction in someone you care about, you must dial down your natural tendency to get nervous and start acting forcefully to counter their attempts to pin you down.

As a Gemini-rising, you will not be seen to be slow to catch on, a poor communicator, or boring, even if you judge yourself to be so.

More than almost any other rising sign, Gemini rising needs to use their innate ability to keep the ideas and communications flowing, despite all obstacles. You can either inspire others or, if the opposite outcome is desired, use your quick mind and command of language to show that your ideas are the best way to go at this time, even if that means deciding not to decide just yet.

CANCER RISING

QUALITY *Cardinal* → | **ELEMENT** *Water* ⬧

It's easy for others to see you as sensitive, shy, caring, and s/mothering, the "s" depending on how strongly you insist that you be obeyed.

....

PHYSICAL APPEARANCE: Medium height; inclined to plumpness; top-heavy figure. Round face; smooth, soft complexion. Eyes often blue or gray. Small hands and feet. Crab-like walk.

FAVORABLE PERSONALITY TRAITS: Domestic, sympathetic, understanding, peaceful, soothing, nurturing, and cheery. With the protective instincts strong, makes a good partner and parent. Respect for tradition. Self-sacrificing.

ADVERSE PERSONALITY TRAITS: Too yielding, sensitive, impressionable. Suffers from hurts and slights, real and imagined. Has a fear of being made to look ridiculous.

....

If you are a Cancer rising, the good news is that you will usually be seen as caring, interested, and someone that people can rely upon. Your ability to help a person, a project, or a business grow through thoughtful and down-to-earth means will be appreciated.

When you are trying to work your will on the world, people may interpret your words and actions as if you are shy about expressing your true beliefs because you have a real emotional connection to the subject at hand. You can be perceived as anywhere from absent, to doing what you can to avoid interacting with harsh or overbearing people and situations, all the way up to being a mother bear for some person or cause you have decided to champion. You are likely to be perceived somewhere on this spectrum even when you are not trying to give this impression.

Remember, however, that some people mistake kindness for weakness and would do anything they can to avoid showing how they feel. Those you encounter who have a negative view of people who are considerate of others—usually because they, themselves, are not considerate and feel judged—may be put off by your Cancer-rising way of interacting with the world, and others may ignore or be inconsiderate of you for the same reason. Even if you are seeking to be a neutral party or to gently nudge people in a particular direction for their own good, problems can arise because Cancer-rising people give others the feeling that they can be themselves, including those who act out because they are emotionally damaged or sick.

Those who have a problem with seeing themselves as shy, passive, or taking into account their feelings or those of others may react to you the way they dialogue with their inner self, getting overly sensitive and emotional with you for no apparent reason.

If you see or even sense this kind of reaction in someone you care about, you must dial down your natural tendency to withdraw completely from this situation. You have a right to live your life as you see fit and to have your needs met and yourself respected.

As a Cancer rising, you will not be seen to be brash, egotistical, or uncaring even if you judge yourself to be so.

More than almost any other rising sign, Cancer rising needs to use their innate ability to help themselves and others feel safe enough to be their authentic self and grow into the person they say they want to become despite all obstacles. Or, if the opposite outcome is desired and you see a person's goals need a course correction, use your emotional intelligence to gently prove, using their own words, that it is your experiences and stories they should take to heart, even if that means abandoning long-held misconceptions.

LEO RISING

QUALITY *Fixed* ◊ | **ELEMENT** *Fire* ◊

It's easy for others to see you as a leader, dramatic and ego-driven with no shyness at all. You seem to be doing great and so no one feels sorry for you. Don't be too familiar.

PHYSICAL APPEARANCE: Average to tall height. Has good posture and an authoritative demeanor. Upper part of body wider than the lower part. Expressive eyes.

FAVORABLE PERSONALITY TRAITS: Loyal, generous, magnanimous, industrious. Executive ability and personal magnetism. Born to rule. Sense of noblesse oblige; fond of children; fun and entertaining.

ADVERSE PERSONALITY TRAITS: "Bossy." Adores adulation; susceptible to flattery. Must be center stage. Exhibitionist complex. Boastful.

If you are a Leo rising, the good news is that you will usually be seen as magnetic, interesting, and fun to be around. Your advice about how to creatively solve a problem will be appreciated.

When you are trying to work your will on the world, people will be inclined to interpret your words and actions as if you expect others to praise you and acknowledge you as their leader; their merely saying "Good idea" will not appear to be enough. You can be perceived on a spectrum, from generously helping others but appearing to make it plain that you want them to show their appreciation, to being quite demonstrative about how you want things to be done, to giving the impression that you are megalomaniacal. As is the nature of the rising sign, you are likely to be perceived somewhere on this spectrum even when you are not trying to give this impression.

Remember, however, that some people mistake self-confidence for self-importance and an overly inflated ego. Those you encounter who have a negative view of people who are proud of themselves, their achievements, and the way they are living life—usually because they are doubtful about their own abilities and whether they are living life to the fullest—may be put off by your Leo-rising way of interacting with the world; others may push back or be inconsiderate of you for the same reason. Even if you are seeking to help someone succeed, come into their full power, or avoid problems and mistakes you have made, problems can arise because Leo-rising people give others the feeling that they are doing what they do because of their own personal needs, especially their need for approval, glorification, and obedience to their leadership.

Those who have a problem with seeing themselves as being the center of attention, judged by their achievements and attributes, or being the person everyone wants to know and spend time with, may react to you the way they dialogue with their inner self, getting overly dramatic and acting out with you for no apparent reason.

If you see or even sense this kind of reaction in someone you care about, you must dial down your natural tendency to act as if everything is a big deal and very important to you. You have a right to live your life as you see fit, to have your needs met and be respected, but be careful that you do not win the battle but lose the war.

As a Leo rising, you will not be seen to be shy, unsure of yourself, or unimportant even if you judge yourself to be so.

More than almost any other rising sign, Leo rising needs to use their innate ability to organize, motivate, and act in service to others. Or, if you see others will not listen to reason, then your acting ability can come into play. No one is more capable of "acting as if . . . were true" than a Leo rising.

VIRGO RISING

QUALITY *Mutable* ≈ | **ELEMENT** *Earth* 🜨

It's easy for others to see you as skilled, fidgety, or worried, no matter how you are feeling. Some may see you as innocent, unjaded, and child-like in a good way.

....

PHYSICAL APPEARANCE: Medium to above-average height. Usually well-formed and active. Round to oval face. Hair, eyes, and complexion tend to be dark.

FAVORABLE PERSONALITY TRAITS: Analytical, excellent conversationalist. Systematic, orderly, and conscientious. Usually on the side of peace. Industrious and practical.

ADVERSE PERSONALITY TRAITS: Critical and complaining. Snobbish and nagging. Too thrifty, becoming cheap. Unwilling to admit having made a mistake.

....

If you are a Virgo rising, the good news is that you will usually be seen as logical, discerning, and an expert analyst. Your appreciation for the little things in life and your knowledge about the details and mechanics of everything that interests you will be appreciated.

When you are trying to accomplish a task you have agreed to take on, people will be inclined to interpret your words and actions as if you are overly concerned with petty or superfluous details and not able to see or be interested in "the big picture." You can be perceived on a spectrum, from appearing merely bored or going through the motions, to appearing to be overthinking the matter at hand, to being so worried and fearful about the outcome and your ability to influence it as to drive yourself to distraction, thereby undermining your own efforts more than anything or anyone could ever do. As is the nature of the rising sign, you are likely to be perceived somewhere on this spectrum even when this is not the case.

Remember, however, that some people are not detail-oriented and prefer to think in broad terms and see things from as high a perspective as possible. Those you encounter who have a negative view of people who are critical thinkers or otherwise give the impression that they are looking for flaws in a system, a product, or a partner may be put off by your Virgo-rising way of interacting with the world. Even if you are seeking to break something down into its component parts so that you can improve it, problems can arise because Virgo-rising people rarely appear to have arrived at the end of their attempt to diagnose a situation or even appear to want to reach a definitive conclusion to that process.

Those who have a problem with seeing themselves as overly fussy or fault-finding, or doubt their ability to correctly analyze a problem and create (and stick to!) a plan, may react to you the way they dialogue with their inner self, getting overly critical and sarcastic with you for no apparent reason.

If you see or even sense this kind of reaction in someone you care about, you must dial down your natural tendency to get anxious and fretful about your ability to do things "the right way" and calmly remember that your best is all that you or anyone can ever do.

As a Virgo rising, you will not be seen to be unskilled, full of yourself, or ignorant even if you judge yourself to be so.

More than almost any other rising sign, Virgo rising needs to use their innate ability to prove the expression "God/dess is in the details," and confine themselves to working at what they are best at, staying in their comfort zone, and showing the rest of us what happens when skill, determination, and hard work are combined in a well-designed work environment. No other rising sign can be as helpful to those who need guidance on how to salvage a difficult situation.

LIBRA RISING

QUALITY *Cardinal* → | ELEMENT *Air* ⇋

It's easy for others to see you as refined, unflappable, and seeking harmony. You can get away with being a bit nasty because others will not see that is what you are doing.

PHYSICAL APPEARANCE: Medium stature; well-formed figure with regular features. Attractive. Skin and hair of smooth texture. Susceptible to plumpness after forty.

FAVORABLE PERSONALITY TRAITS: Sociable, good-natured, talented, and artistic. Always ready to grant a favor. Excels as fashion or beauty experts. Somewhat easy-going—dislikes discord—but can take a firm stand.

ADVERSE PERSONALITY TRAITS: Likely to become a "yes" man or woman. Lacks backbone. Evasive and occasionally too subtle. Indifferent, because of inability to feel emotions strongly.

If you are a Libra rising, the good news is that you will usually be seen as attractive, refined, and a skilled negotiator. Your appreciation for the beauty in life and your interest in bringing peace, love, and balance to the world will be highly regarded.

When you are trying to accomplish a task you have agreed to take on, people will be inclined to interpret your words and actions as if you are overly concerned with seeking a consensus or compromise based on bouncing your ideas off the other people involved, rather than because you are decided and all-in on a particular outcome. You can be perceived on a spectrum, from deciding not to decide, to agreeing with things you do not really agree with to avoid disharmony or harshness, to appearing to be completely undecided regarding the matter at hand despite obviously knowing well both sides of an argument, to being willing to do whatever it takes to achieve your goal the way you envision it, including acting aggressively. Aggression is not something usually associated with Libra, but many military generals are Libras, willing to fight for peace. As is the nature of the rising sign, you are likely to be perceived somewhere on this spectrum even when you are not trying to give this impression.

Remember, however, that some people are not interested in the way things look, whether that is people's physical appearance, their reputation, or public relations images. Some people's default method is to do whatever it takes to get the job done, even if it is not pretty or leaves a bad taste in people's mouths. No Libra rising would ever appear to want to make things more disharmonious, even if that were their aim. This is the nature of the rising sign.

Those you encounter who have a negative view of people who appear to be noble or elegant, or otherwise give the impression that they are somehow better than other people, may be put off by your Libra-rising way of interacting with the world. Even if you are simply trying to be one of the blessed peacemakers, problems can arise because Libra-rising people have to work extra hard to appear to be decisive enough to work well with those who have opinions set in stone and who have a strong distrust of others. Libra is a goal-oriented sign that is only comfortable being in the middle of a situation weighing the various components, like the balance scale that is its symbol, so appearing to be decisive takes work for you.

Those who have a problem with seeing themselves as looking attractive or being fair, or who doubt their ability to make a decision without the input of "their betters," may react to you the way they dialogue with their inner self, getting angry with you for not agreeing with them or for seeing both sides of the issue.

If you see or even sense this kind of reaction in someone you care about, you must dial down your natural tendency to show that you see the justice in both sides of the matter at hand and make a special effort to show that you know how to be a fair and kind partner who treats others as equals.

As a Libra rising, you will not be seen to be harsh, cruel, or overly opinionated even if you judge yourself to be so.

More than almost any other rising sign, Libra rising needs to use their innate ability to help other people arrive at a decision that is beyond questioning—yes, you can do that!—but to do it in a way that requires you to walk the line between model citizen and counterculture subversive, adapting the rules so they can be used as tools to achieve goals. No other rising sign can be as helpful and respected a counselor to those who have lost their sense of perspective about life and how to live it successfully as Libra rising.

SCORPIO RISING

QUALITY *Fixed* ◊ | ELEMENT *Water* ◐

It's easy for others to see you as seductive, hard to read, and judgmental. You appear to see others' secrets and flaws and that makes it easy for you to be misunderstood.

PHYSICAL APPEARANCE: Medium height or below; usually heavy-set body; forceful appearance. Coloring is dark; hair thick and eyebrows prominent. Intense gaze.

FAVORABLE PERSONALITY TRAITS: Strong willpower. Can barge through obstacles. Ambitious and faithful to friends. Intense, deep, courageous, and can put up a fight for a cause.

ADVERSE PERSONALITY TRAITS: Jealous, dominating, and unscrupulous. Often uses any means to gain an end. Ruthless. Quick to anger, hot for revenge. Greedy.

If you are a Scorpio rising, the good news is that you will usually be seen as sexy, mysterious, and someone not to be trifled with. Your ability to see to the heart of any matter, to keep and detect secrets, and to uncover lies, plots, and cover-ups of all kinds will be appreciated.

It is important for you to remember that people who are for some reason not being their authentic selves or who are uncomfortable in their own skin will be inclined to interpret your words and actions as if you are seeing right through their self-deceit and judging them wanting, as they, themselves, do consciously or unconsciously. You can be perceived on a spectrum, from looking right through other people as if they were not there, to saying the right words at the right time to almost magically make a person aware of what they are actually saying and doing despite what they have intended to say and do, to being seen as so judgmental that you appear to condemn the other people's words and actions in preparation for cutting them out of your life. As is the nature of the rising sign, you are likely to be perceived somewhere on this spectrum even when this is not the case.

Remember, however, that some people are not as strong as they appear and are therefore unable to handle the powerful gaze and apparent judgment of a Scorpio rising. The sensuous quality of a Scorpio rising adds the element of a person's sexual attraction and proclivities to every encounter and can further throw a person off balance and render them unable to accurately determine what you are trying to say or do. Some people's default method is to avoid their "dark side" at all costs, as if all people do not share this very human quality. To someone who is suffering from past traumas, feeling uncertain, or in a confused state, it would be easy to misinterpret a Scorpio rising's self-contained and powerful presentation to the world as somehow disrespectful.

Those you encounter who have a negative view of people who appear to be secretive, who are comfortable with their sexuality, or who do not engage in small talk but only speak when they have something they consider to be important to say, may be put off by your Scorpio-rising way of interacting with the world. Even if you are simply thinking about your own situation and its mundane problems, problems can arise because Scorpio-rising people have to work extra hard to appear to be kind, friendly, and interested in others who present themselves in a superficial manner.

Those who have a problem with being comfortable about their own sexuality and sexuality in general, or who have secrets that they will do anything to avoid being revealed, may react to you the way they dialogue with their inner self, giving you the silent treatment and acting inappropriately with you for no apparent reason.

If you see or even sense this kind of reaction in someone you care about, you must become aware of your natural tendency to always mind your own business, experiencing life on the deepest, most profound, and beyond words level and make a special effort to show that you are or can be totally committed to being there for them and to using your seemingly magical powers for their benefit.

As a Scorpio rising, you will not be seen to be unattractive, indecisive, or ineffectual even if you judge yourself to be so.

More than almost any other rising sign, Scorpio rising needs to use their innate ability to penetrate all illusions and get to the heart of every matter, even if they cannot use the information obtained. No other rising sign can be as helpful and respected a detective in revealing truths that need revealing. Scorpio risings will never reveal their secrets unless and until it is the right time to do so.

SAGITTARIUS RISING

QUALITY *Mutable* ≈ | ELEMENT *Fire* 🔥

It's easy for others to see you as truthful and philosophical. You can often feel like you are a stranger in a strange land, even if you never leave your hometown.

· ·

PHYSICAL APPEARANCE: Tall to medium figure. Long or oval face. Ruddy complexion and hair of varying shades. Eyes unusually expressive. Looks like a combination of many ethnicities.

FAVORABLE PERSONALITY TRAITS: Frank, honest, loyal, and unselfish. A lucky idealist. Psychic and engenders faith and inspiration wherever needed. A great sense of humor.

ADVERSE PERSONALITY TRAITS: Too frank for your own good. Restless and cannot commit. Rash and oversensitive. Irresponsible. More interested in the hunt than in the capture.

· ·

If you are a Sagittarius rising, the good news is that you will usually be seen as honest, broad-minded, and both knowledgeable about and respectful of the various cultures around the world even if you do not agree with significant aspects of their way of life. Your desire to learn from the best practices of the world's many peoples and to adapt these concepts for yourself will be appreciated.

It is important for you to remember that people who are narrow-minded and would love a world where everyone thinks, acts, and lives the same way they do will be inclined to interpret your words

RISING SIGNS

and your actions as if you were trying to put undue pressure on them to step out of their comfort zone and try to accept new ways of thinking and living. You can be perceived on a spectrum, from giving the impression that you are not in sync with the cultural mores you grew up with, to learning another language or experimenting with different ways of living, to being seen as having a lack of respect for those who have refused to expand their understanding of some aspect of life or who choose to ignore truths you believe to be self-evident. As is the nature of the rising sign, you are likely to be perceived somewhere on this spectrum even when you are not trying to give this impression.

Remember, however, that some people cannot handle the blunt honesty of a Sagittarius rising. The Sagittarius rising gives the appearance of being committed to speaking the truth even when such honesty is detrimental to them and their purpose. To further complicate matters, Sagittarius risings are legendary for blurting out secrets and usually at the worst possible time. Some people cannot handle the truth spoken at any time. The old saying "The truth hurts" is all too true for most people, even some Sagittarius risings.

Those you encounter who have a negative view of people who appear to be overly philosophical, long-winded, and not sure of what they believe, or who are tolerant or actively supportive of "foreign" views and beliefs, or who seem to worship the flora and fauna of nature will not be comfortable watching your unique fiery enthusiasm for life. Even if you are simply trying to give your honest opinion, either because you have been asked for it or because you think giving it will help someone, problems can arise because Sagittarius rising people have to work extra hard to appear respectful and accepting of those who appear rigid in their beliefs. Without giving this respect, Sagittarius rising will not have a meaningful dialogue with those who appear unjust in their attitude toward others and disrespectful of those who consider themselves to be seekers of truth and justice.

Those who have a problem with allowing another person to be themselves fully, to be free to say and do what they feel is right at the moment, or who are committed to lifelong learning and change their beliefs when they have obtained the evidence that they were wrong and now are closer to "the Truth," may react to you the way they dialogue with their inner self, acting tactless and saying words that they will regret for no apparent reason.

If you see or even sense this kind of reaction in someone you care about, you must become aware of your natural tendency to let the world in on your inner dialogue and make a special effort to show that you are as interested in another person's journey as you are your own and that your appearing to be committed to conflicting beliefs is part of your effort to arrive at the Truth, a goal you assume is shared by all.

As a Sagittarius rising, you will not be seen to be unjust, closed-minded, or prejudiced even if you judge yourself to be so.

More than almost any other rising sign, Sagittarius rising needs to use their innate ability to seek, communicate, and establish truth, justice, and fairness in service to others. No other rising sign can be as powerful an example of what being true to oneself can accomplish.

CAPRICORN RISING

QUALITY *Cardinal* → | ELEMENT *Earth* 🜨

It's easy for others to see you as serious, extremely competent, and a "wet blanket" when they want to do things you disapprove of. You seem to become younger as you get older.

....

PHYSICAL APPEARANCE: Height is average. Defined bones and teeth. Thick hair. Chiseled features, not always regular. Dignified gait.

FAVORABLE PERSONALITY TRAITS: Reliable, capable, ambitious, and patient. Gains wisdom through experience. Thrifty. Successful organizer. Respects tradition and those in prominent places.

ADVERSE PERSONALITY TRAITS: Melancholy. Pessimistic; influenced by head instead of heart. Stingy. Tendency to toady to the top; overbearing with the underdog. Yearns for power.

....

If you are a Capricorn rising, the good news is that you will usually be seen as a no-nonsense person deserving of respect, and both knowledgeable and respectful of the laws, rules, and traditions of whatever you concern yourself with, even if you do not agree with significant parts of them. Your desire to do what is necessary to achieve recognition and success as you define it will usually be appreciated.

It is important for you to remember that people who are not happy with things the way they are and especially with those in authority will be inclined to interpret your words and your actions as though you are trying to put undue pressure on them to stop "complaining" and do what they know deep down they have to do and not just what they want to do. You can be perceived on a spectrum, from giving the impression that you are excessively mulling over something that you are not satisfied with, to appearing to want to correct others by parroting the words of people you respect or who are in authority and can help you on your path to becoming an authority, to being seen as so negative or taciturn as to make others worry that you are clinically depressed. As is the nature of the rising sign, you are likely to be perceived somewhere on this spectrum even when this is not the case.

Remember, however, that some people cannot handle the disciplined seriousness of a Capricorn rising. The Capricorn rising gives the appearance of being disapproving of those who are only interested in doing things the easy or fun way, though this usually takes the form of sarcasm or dark humor. To further complicate matters, Capricorn risings are often perceived as attempting to "rain on people's parade," when they are simply trying to overcome their own desire to join the fun because they are concerned it will somehow detract from what needs to be accomplished.

Those you encounter who have a negative view of people who appear to be cautious, too concerned with their career, or more comfortable going by the book will not give you the level of respect you deserve. Even if you are simply trying to get the job done so you can move on, problems can arise because Capricorn-rising people have to work extra hard to avoid appearing to be trying to make others look less conscientious, hardworking, or committed to the common cause. Without getting the respect they deserve, Capricorn-rising will be unable to appear pleased even if goals are accomplished and targets are met.

Those who have a problem delegating or who overburden themselves and others with more work and responsibilities than a person in their situation should be expected to accomplish, and especially those who were given too much responsibility as children, may react to you the way they dialogue with their inner self, acting like they are your teacher or superior to you for no apparent reason.

If you see or even sense this kind of reaction in someone you care about, you must become aware of your natural tendency to not let others see that you, too, are burdened by tedium and overwork and make a special effort to show that you are a part of the group. Make it clear that, although you may appear to be doing so only because it would be good for you, you are just tired and overworked.

As a Capricorn rising, you will not be seen to be lazy, unambitious, or frivolous even if you judge yourself to be so.

More than almost any other rising sign, Capricorn rising needs to use their innate ability to plan, execute that plan, and establish something that can survive the test of time to build relationships. No other rising sign understands the harsh realities of life and how important emotional support is, even though Capricorn as a sign is not usually associated with deep emotional needs. Remember that the sign's symbol is a mountain goat with a fish's tail, and in astrology, fish and water have to do with emotion.

AQUARIUS RISING

QUALITY *Fixed* ◊ | ELEMENT *Air* ♒

It's easy for others to see you as inventive, emotionally detached, and eccentric. You love humanity, but it's people who can often annoy you because they fight the future.

PHYSICAL APPEARANCE: Usually of medium stature; compact build, but well formed. Oval face. Eyes, hair, and complexion vary. A strong speaking voice. Magnetic and inspiring appearance.

FAVORABLE PERSONALITY TRAITS: Understanding and humane. Often far ahead of their time. Kindhearted and helpful. Happy when asked for a favor. Communicative.

ADVERSE PERSONALITY TRAITS: Temperamental, unreasonable, and contrary. Always out of tune and out of step with associates. Loves to stir up trouble; delights in rebellion.

If you are an Aquarius rising, the good news is that you will usually be seen as cool, calm, and different enough to fit in well with the new normal of being a unique individual who wants to get on with the business of bringing the future forward. Your honesty about your desire to do what is necessary to achieve this future as you define it will usually be appreciated.

It is important for you to remember that people who are not happy with things changing too quickly or in too many ways will be inclined to interpret your words and actions as if you were trying to put undue

RISING SIGNS

pressure on them to radically alter their lives to a degree that they know they cannot live with comfortably. You can be perceived on a spectrum, from pleasantly eccentric, to appearing to be committed to "being the change you want to see," or the model citizen for the new age you are trying to bring forward, to being seen as dangerously out of touch with reality. As is the nature of the rising sign, you are likely to be perceived somewhere on this spectrum even when you are not trying to give this impression.

Remember, however, that some people cannot handle the apparent uninterest in the often-profound disruptive consequences of the plans for change coming from an Aquarius rising. They often give the appearance of being unemotional to the point of being perceived as more than a little robotic. To further complicate matters, Aquarian risings are often perceived as the amplification of the oddest aspects of their sun and moon signs, but not always, adding an element of "What are they going to say or do now?" to their interactions with others.

Those you encounter who have a negative view of people who appear to be uncaringly rebellious, too concerned with the past and the future but not concerned enough with the present, will not feel comfortable in your presence. Even if you are simply trying to be a person who is the living embodiment of marching to your own drummer and being your authentic self, doing your best to throw off the shackles of a past whose lessons are no longer applicable for the future you wish to see manifested on Earth, problems can arise because Aquarius risings have to work extra hard to appear like they have an emotional connection or even a more than superficial interest in other people. Without getting the admiration for their fearless individualism and respect for their unorthodox beliefs, Aquarius risings will be unable to appear as though they want to get to know another person well.

Those who have a problem with people who seem to be going out of their way to show the world how unusual, unconventional, and unconcerned about what other people think about them and their way of living may react to you the way they dialogue with their inner self, acting cold and distant with you for no apparent reason.

If you see or even sense this kind of reaction in someone you care about, you must become aware of your natural tendency to not let others see that you, too, are affected by your emotions and the suffering of other beings. You'll need to make a special effort to show that you do, in fact, care about other people but sometimes get lost in your head and your desire to envision a future where their problems are solvable.

As an Aquarius rising, you will not be seen to be ordinary, dull, or overly emotional even if you judge yourself to be so.

More than almost any other rising sign, Aquarius rising needs to use their innate ability to innovate and think outside of the box. Most people do not get a chance to have their new invention or way of doing something change the world, and so changing their world has to be enough to keep them going. No other rising sign understands what it takes to formulate a plan that can eliminate conditions of the past that should no longer be allowed to exist and to then implement that plan. Like its symbol, the old man pouring out water for all to drink, Aquarius-rising people need to be satisfied with just getting their ideas out there for those thirsty for their version of the future.

PISCES RISING

QUALITY *Mutable* ≈ | ELEMENT *Water* 💧

It's easy for others to see you as listening to a psychic voice or, alternatively, as if something is wrong. What you are experiencing at the soul level shows on your face.

PHYSICAL APPEARANCE: Well-proportioned with smaller limbs. Fleshy face and body. Glowing skin. Artistic fingers. Large, dreamy eyes.

FAVORABLE PERSONALITY TRAITS: Charming, sympathetic, and agreeable. Loves beauty and delights in art. Champion of the underdog. Capable of inspirational achievement.

ADVERSE PERSONALITY TRAITS: Timid, weak, and supersensitive. Enjoys the role of the martyr. Talkative. Inferiority complex. Resorts to camouflage.

If you are a Pisces rising, the good news is that you will usually be seen as a sensitive, compassionate, and caring person. Your desire to do what you can to help individuals in need will usually be appreciated.

It is important for you to remember that people who are not comfortable with those who appear to be overly selfless and willing to give people the shirt off their backs will be inclined to interpret your words and actions as if you are trying to put undue pressure on them to be more understanding, forgiving, and charitable to those they may not want to help. You can be perceived on a spectrum, from giving the impression that you are a caring person, to appearing to want to be part of an organization or movement dedicated to helping those in need, to being seen as so desirous of living in a better world that you are willing to sacrifice yourself in some way, either as a selfless charitable worker or as an addict to substances and behaviors that take you out of this world and into one where your pain seems to be dulled. As is the nature of the rising sign, you are likely to be perceived somewhere on this spectrum even when this is not the case.

Remember, however, that some people cannot handle the disturbingly moody behavior of a Pisces rising. Pisces rising gives the appearance of being lost in psychic connection, seemingly hearing voices from somewhere that others do not hear. This can make other people think that there is something wrong, that the Pisces rising is upset or unhappy either with them or because of some unknown cause. To further complicate matters, Pisces risings are often perceived

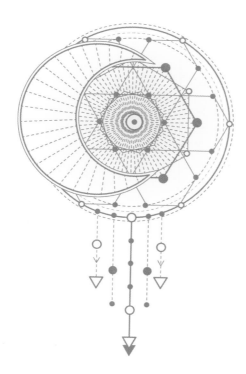

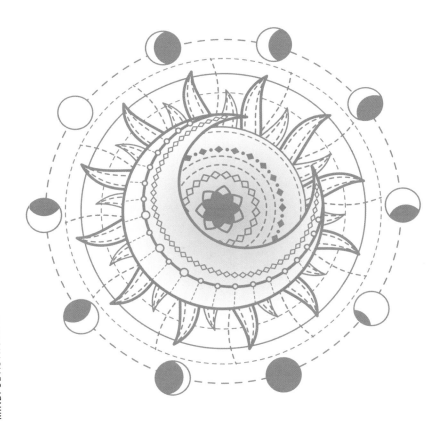

as overly sensitive and delicate when they are actually stronger than most people because their faith and seeking connection with the unseen world give them true metaphysical fitness.

Those you encounter who have a negative view of people who appear to be ready to sacrifice their own interests or otherwise disrupt their daily routine for the good of another will not give you the level of respect you deserve. Even if you are simply trying to stay true to your beliefs, problems can arise because Pisces risings have to work extra hard to appear like they are not trying to make others look less spiritual, humane, and devoted to their religious obligations. This is going to be further complicated by the fact that Pisces rising people will always have that "I'm listening to you but also to my inner voice" look.

Those who have a problem with caring, spiritual people who ask a lot of personal questions in their desire to help understand how best they can be of service may react to you the way they dialogue with their inner self, acting hurt and demoralized for no apparent reason.

If you see or even sense this kind of reaction in someone you care about, you must become aware of your natural tendency to see someone who needs help as having asked you for help and instead wait for them to request assistance before you go into your default way of interacting with people.

As a Pisces rising, you will not be seen to be uncaring, miserly, or selfish even if you judge yourself to be so.

More than almost any other rising sign, Pisces rising needs to use their innate ability to truly connect with people to feel fully alive. No other rising sign understands loneliness, fragility, and the tenuous connections shared by all beings as you do. Remember that Pisces's symbol is two fish, each swimming in opposite directions, so do not be surprised when you are seen quite differently by people who know you best—sometimes in seeming exaltation and sometimes in seeming anguish. Only a Pisces rising can allow both energies to exist in themselves at the same time, a rare feat, as Pisces is the rarest of the rising signs.

Understanding Your Celestial Trilogy

DEVELOPING **AN AWARENESS** of your sun, moon, and rising signs allows you to be truly mindful of your unique characteristics, feelings, and projections, as well as those of other important people in your life. Finding peace of mind begins with self-reflection to gain perspective on your goals, your emotions, and your reactions to what life throws at you, a vital life skill at this most unusual time in history. In order to understand a person as a whole, getting to know their sun, moon, and rising signs is crucial.

TO REITERATE

YOUR SUN SIGN: Describes your basic nature and motivations, the core of who you are

YOUR MOON SIGN: Rules your emotions and sensitivities, your deep, inward nature

YOUR RISING SIGN: Influences your style and appearance and the way other people perceive you

Your sun, moon, and rising signs form what we call your "celestial trilogy," three stories that form a three-dimensional portrait of you, one that gives depth and nuance to whatever level of astrological wisdom you have attained (and if you have read this far, consider yourself a budding astrologer!). Understanding how they work together can give you insights into why you do the things you do, how you feel, and how others view you. This combination of energies is a large part of what makes us all unique. Here is our guide for putting it all together.

IF YOUR SUN, MOON, AND RISING SIGNS ARE
ALL THE SAME SIGN OF THE ZODIAC

If your sun, moon, and rising signs are all the same sign of the zodiac, then you are what is known as a "triple" Aries, Taurus, or whatever sign you have been blessed to call yours. You are just about the purest example of your sign possible and with you, what you see is what you get to a level not known by the rest of us. You do not have to concern yourself with blending two or more signs harmoniously, only with blending the various aspects of your sign's meanings. You will, however, have to contend with a world in which almost everyone else has a more complex, complicated, and often conflicted way of thinking, feeling, and doing what they do.

IF YOUR SUN, MOON, AND RISING SIGNS ARE ALL THE SAME QUALITY (EITHER CARDINAL, FIXED, OR MUTABLE)

If your sun, moon, and rising signs are all the same quality (see pages 28–29), either cardinal, fixed, or mutable, then you, too, are a pure blend but of a different way of living. If you are all cardinal signs, then you are goal-oriented to a degree that most other people will find difficult to understand. If you are all fixed signs, then you are stubborn and will not want to change anything in your life, especially your beliefs—unless you finally come to the conclusion that you are wrong and there is something better that is attainable for you. If you are all mutable signs, then you are flexible and changeable to the point where it may be difficult for others, or even you, to know what your core beliefs are. As it is with having one's sun, moon, and rising signs all in the same sign of the zodiac, you, too, will have to contend with a world in which almost everyone does not so totally subscribe to either a goal-oriented, stubborn, or changeable way to live daily life as do you.

IF YOUR SUN, MOON, AND RISING SIGNS ARE ALL IN THE SAME ELEMENT, EITHER FIRE, AIR, WATER, OR EARTH

If your sun, moon, and rising signs are all the same element (see page 142), either fire, air, water, or earth, then you, too, are a unique and pure blend of ways to approach daily existence. If you have your celestial trilogy in fire, then you are a person to whom taking action, having faith, and always being truthful are ways of being that come naturally to you. If it is in the element of air, then you dwell in the realm of ideas, theories, and concepts of how things are and how they could be. If your celestial trilogy is in the element of water, then your world is one dominated by feelings, emotions, and intuitions that are usually beyond words and beyond the realm of logical thought. Finally, if your sun, moon, and rising signs are in the element of earth, then you live in the real world and understand its beauty, bounty, and limits more than others could ever know.

IF YOU HAVE ANY TWO PIECES OF YOUR CELESTIAL TRILOGY IN ANY SIGN, QUALITY, OR ELEMENT

If you have any two pieces of your celestial trilogy in the same sign, quality, or element, then you should pay particular attention to those two pieces—sun and moon, sun and rising sign, or moon and rising sign—and the meanings associated with the sign, quality, or element they share. Compare those meanings with the meanings associated with the sign, quality, or element of that third piece of your celestial trilogy and you will see if there is a harmonious synergy of its three pieces or if the meanings conflict or cancel each other out. If there is conflict or canceling out, you can use your favorite strengths from each piece to help you counteract or compensate for the aspects of your personality with which you are not comfortable.

IF YOUR CELESTIAL TRILOGY IS ANY COMBINATION OF FIRE, AIR, WATER

You have been gifted with the ability to take action to bring the ideas you have into reality through your ability to have an emotional connection with those you care about, either those you cherish or those who are important to the attaining of your goals. Be aware that you must try extra hard to apply your harmonized, logical mind and emotional intelligence to a plan of action you are considering before you actually embark upon it with the goal of this prior consideration being to make sure that what you are about to do with your precious time on earth is practical to attain and useful to enough people if it is attained.

IF YOUR CELESTIAL TRILOGY IS ANY COMBINATION OF FIRE, AIR, EARTH

You have been gifted with the ability to take action to bring into reality any ideas you have for improving your reality and that of other people. You do not have to pre-plan when it comes to the practicality and usefulness of what you are about to do. You do, however, have to make a special effort to understand how your actions and the implementation of your ideas are going to affect other people on an emotional level. Be aware that other people's feelings about what you do can assist or inhibit the realization of your goals as much as available resources and the purely practical considerations involved with executing your plans.

IF YOUR CELESTIAL TRILOGY IS ANY COMBINATION OF FIRE, WATER, EARTH

You have been gifted with the ability to take action to bring into reality the things you believe you need to have the life you want to be living. Your actions will be guided by your intuitive understanding and emotional connection to anyone involved in your efforts. You do, however, have to make a special effort to make sure that the actions you take are being guided by your own ideas about how things should be and are not allowing the ideas of others to override your own. Be aware that other people's ideas may have more to do with their own needs and wants and not enough to do with yours.

IF YOUR CELESTIAL TRILOGY IS ANY COMBINATION OF AIR, WATER, EARTH

You have been gifted with the ability to experience, examine, and connect to the real world and the rest of humanity on a deep and profound level. You have a balanced understanding of what it means to be a human being who is inextricably tied to the natural world and of how to best take care of its resources for this and future generations. You do, however, have to make a special effort to turn your ideas, intuitions, and plans into actions that bring them to fruition. Be aware that other people may not need regular periods of rest and recharge and that includes the recharging of your faith in yourself and the rightness of your cause.

The best way—in fact, the only way—for you to understand this unique blend, your personal celestial trinity, is to first become aware of it, which you have now done, and then to see how what we have written stacks up against who you are. Our purpose in life is to grow and love and bring ourselves into balance, with self-awareness. The practice of mindfulness can serve us well on our journey to happiness and peace. And, with the help of astrology, we have the ability to really see ourselves and others.

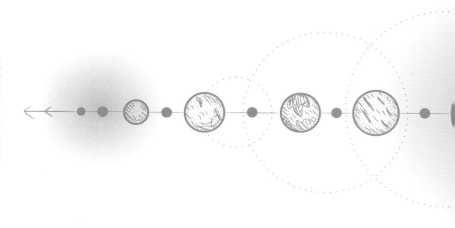

We can learn to pay attention in the moment, recognizing and acknowledging behaviors, feelings, and thoughts, embracing our totality. Then we can choose to express the highest frequency of these energies in a realized and responsible manner.

We know full well that no one knows you like you know yourself. What we have written is the essence of what we have learned after our decades of astrological practice, presented in a form that you can take into your inner dialogue and see how it resonates with who you now know yourself to be. If we have done our jobs correctly, then *Mindful Astrology* can be your companion in self-understanding and self-empowerment throughout the rest of your life.

Wishing you love, light, and laughter always, and in all ways,
Amy Zerner & Monte Farber

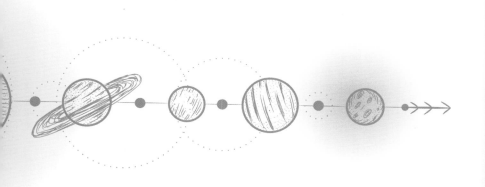

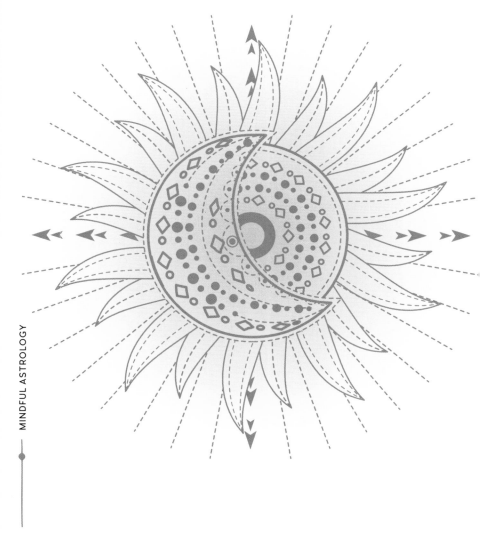

ABOUT THE AUTHORS

AMY ZERNER and **MONTE FARBER** are the world's foremost designers of interactive spiritual inner-guidance teaching systems, more commonly known today as "divination systems" or "oracles." Since 1988, their creations have helped millions of people around the world in eighteen languages get in touch with their Higher Self as they learned astrology, tarot card reading, and numerous other ancient wisdom teachings, which Zerner and Farber have updated for the twenty-first century, thereby satisfying Monte's Aquarius sun sign.

Amy is also a National Endowment for the Arts award-winning fine artist for her pioneering (Amy is an Aries!) fabric collage tapestry paintings and a fashion designer whose Spiritual Couture™ jackets, caftans, and separates have been sold exclusively by Bergdorf Goodman and Neiman Marcus for the past twenty years. The couple lives on the East End of Long Island with their beloved shaman cat, Zane, a perfect example of mindfulness, to whom this book is dedicated.

Some of their best-selling titles are: *The Enchanted Tarot, Karma Cards, The Creativity Oracle, The Chakra Meditation Kit, Little Reminders: Law of Attraction, Astrology for Wellness, The Enchanted Love Tarot, The Enchanted Spellboard, Sun Sign Secrets, Instant Tarot, Quantum Affirmations, The Soulmate Path, The Psychic Circle, Signs & Seasons: An Astrology Cookbook,* and *The Wild Goddess Oracle.*

Visit their websites TheEnchantedWorld.com, AmyZerner.com, and MonteFarber.com.

ENDORSEMENTS FOR MINDFUL ASTROLOGY

"Wonder how you might create a balanced, soulful life? Look no further than your astrology chart. When you understand your astrological makeup, you're more likely to make decisions that are for your highest good. Beloved authors Amy Zerner and Monte Farber share their wisdom in *Mindful Astrology*, a deep dive into the sun, moon, and ascendant, the three main points in the natal chart. This cosmic trio offers insights into your personal strengths and vulnerabilities, which can lead to greater awareness of how you operate. Learning to work with your celestial blueprint is the first step to an empowered life. Every astrology enthusiast will find this beautiful book the perfect companion on their self-discovery journey."—Theresa Reed, author of *Astrology for Real Life: A Workbook for Beginners*

"If you want to be able to understand the basics of your soul personality and learn how those basics can help you to find acceptance and peace of mind, this is the book for you! Amy and Monte's usual refreshing and fun style with easy to understand descriptions makes this a must-have for anyone that wants to know themselves on a deeper level."—Louise Edington, Cosmic Owl Astrology

"*Mindful Astrology* offers insights for each sun sign into love and relationships, work and career, and wealth and success. It also provides tips for working with your natal celestial energies to bring greater balance and fulfillment into your life. Handsomely designed with full-color graphics, this introduction to the ancient art of astrology, written by two of America's most respected metaphysicians, is a must-have for beginning stargazers."—Skye Alexander, author of *Magickal Astrology* and *The Modern Witchcraft Book of Tarot*

"Monte Farber and Amy Zerner are masters of their craft; not only providing beautiful wisdom and teachings, but also a breadth of artistry and playfulness which is essential at this time of awakening."—Simran Singh, publisher of *11:11 Magazine* and 11:11 Talk Radio host and author

"Another winner from the cosmic couple who have helped millions divine their way on their life paths." —Colette Baron-Reid, intuition expert and internationally bestselling author

"*Mindful Astrology* is another brilliant gift from the divination luminaries Monte Farber and Amy Zerner. Filled with profound, life-enhancing wisdom that is easily accessible for anyone interested in astrology, *Mindful Astrology* will radically transform your relationship with yourself and the larger world around you."

—Shaheen Miro, author of *Lunar Alchemy: Everyday Moon Magic to Transform Your Life* and *The Uncommon Tarot*

"As a bookstore owner, I can honestly say that any book by Monte Farber and Amy Zerner never disappoints. In fact, books by this dynamic duo sell the minute we get them in stock. So, ready...set...go...buy it the minute you can! *Mindful Astrology* does not disappoint. In fact, this book is so timely. It helps us navigate our lives just when we need it most! *Mindful Astrology* gives us so much more than just what our sun sign is each month. It helps us understand our holistic, celestial self. This book is approachable to those new to astrology, but is also stimulating to those who are more advanced in astrology. In other words, it is time for all to be mindful of our entire cosmic selves."

—Michelle Welch, owner of SoulTopia, LLC and author of *The Magic of Connection*